Riding Memory's Chariot

By the same author:

- Crisis in Law Enforcement
- Human Rights and Law Enforcement
- Law Enforcement and Cross Border Terrorism
- Reflections and Reminiscences of Police Officer
- Terrorism Around the World: Challenges and Responses
- Trafficking in Women and Children: Myths and Realities
- Violent Neighbourhood Turbulence in Pakistan and Afghanistan

---

About the Author

Sankar Sen is presently a senior fellow at the Institute of Social Sciences, New Delhi. He is a distinguished member of the India Police Service allotted to Odisha Cadre. He served in the Intelligence Bureau for 7-years and also served as the Director, National Police Academy, Hyderabad and Director General of National Human Rights Commission. He is deeply involved in the human rights sensitization of the Indian police and personnel of para military forces and improvement of prison administration. He was awarded the Police Medal for Meritorious Service as well as President's Medal for Distinguished Service. His articles on law enforcement, terrorism, human rights, custodial justice, trafficking in women and children etc. regularly appear in national dailies and well-known magazines in and outside the country. He has authored many books, including, Indian Police Today, Human Rights in Developing Society, Human Rights and Inhuman Wrongs, Enforcing Police Accountability through Civilian Oversight, Tryst with Law Enforcement and Human Rights.

Riding Memory's Chariot

Sankar Sen

CONCEPT PUBLISHING COMPANY PVT. LTD.
NEW DELHI-110059

ISBN-13: 978-93-5125-165-1

First Published 2015

Published and Printed by

Concept
Since 1974

Concept Publishing Company Pvt. Ltd.
A/15-16, Commercial Block, Mohan Garden
New Delhi-110059 (India)
T: 25351460, 25351794, *F*: 091-11-25357109
E: publishing@conceptpub.com, W: www.conceptpub.com
Editorial Office: H-13, Bali Nagar, New Delhi-110 015, India.

Cataloging in Publication Data--Courtesy: D.K. Agencies (P) Ltd. <docinfo@dkagencies.com>

Sen, Sankar, 1936- **author.**
Riding memory's chariot / Sankar Sen.
pages cm
Includes index.
ISBN 9789351251651

1. Police--India--Biography. 2. India--Biography. I. Title.

DDC 363.2092254 23

Nadoja Dr. Justice V.S. Malimath
Former
Chief Justice of Karnataka & Kerala,
Chairman, Central Administrative Tribunal,
Member, National Human Rights Commission,
Chairman, Committee on Reforms of Criminal Justice System,
Chairman, Law Commission of Karnataka.

"Shantiniketan"
Palace Loop Road,
Vasanthanagar,
Bangalore – 560 052.

Foreword

I am very happy to be called upon to pen my foreword to this unique book containing excellent articles written by my esteemed friend Sri. Sankar Sen on a variety of topics of great relevance to our fast changing society. It is his deep concern for the welfare of the society that appears to be the chief motivating force behind each of the articles.

Sri Sankar Sen has acquired a formidable reputation as one of the most efficient Director of National Police Academy at Hyderabad. He is a recipient of many honours and Medals for his outstanding service to the nation. When the National Human Rights Commission was established under the Protection of Human Rights Act in 1993, Justice Ranganath Mishra the first Chairman of the National Human Rights Commission and former Chief Justice of India picked him for the prestigious position of Director General of Investigation of the Commission. It is when I joined the Commission as a Member that we had the opportunity of working together in protecting and promoting Human Rights of the people. He worked with great passion, commitment and tact in redressing the grievances of victims of violation of Human Rights. This was possible because he was able to secure willing cooperation of the Police personnel, the NGOs and the general public.

Sri. Sankar Sen is deeply committed to the philosophy of Human Rights. He is a kind and sensitive person, who is genuinely concerned about the welfare of the society. He is constantly involved in finding ways and means to prevent invasion of Human Rights of innocent persons. It is this concern that finds expression in many of these articles. This compilation contains articles he has written about the great personalities that have inspired him, as a token of his gratitude. The pen portraits of the stalwarts that he had opportunity to come in contact with are quite impressive.

The compilation is far from a lifeless and boring treatise. The variety of topics covered by the author and the lucid style of presentation would hold the interest of everyone interested in life and living. Sri. Sankar Sen is a highly cultured person and a great humanist. He loves life and admires goodness wherever he finds.

I would like to compliment the author for his commendable work with the famous quote from Bharthruhari....

> *"Neither the bracelet nor the glittering shiny;*
> *No sand paste, no floral decoration after death;*
> *Not even the wearing of turban by man;*
> *Only the words of mouth of a cultured man do remain ornaments;*
> *All other embellishments vanish in truth;*
> *only the power of spoken words will remain an eternal adoration."*

(Nadoja Dr. Justice V.S. Malimath)

Contents

Introduction

Invincible time moves on relentlessly and waits for none. Past and present merge and inexorably move towards the future. As I look back wistfully on the bygone years, many events of the past, both bright and melancholy, crowd my mind. Out of the mists of the past arise before my mind's eye some towering figures of Indian police with whom I have had the opportunity to come in close touch and draw from them visions and inspiration. I admired their unflinching commitment to the profession and charismatic leadership qualities. I also had the wonderful opportunity of working with some of the finest judicial minds of the country during my innings in the National Human Rights Commission. I have tried to draw brief pen-portraits of some of these stalwarts and recall the flavour of their personalities and the impact they had on me.

I have further briefly narrated some of the interesting and amusing episodes of my official career, which typified the warts and all of our public life. They are symptomatic of the inadequacies of our administration, particularly, in the realm of criminal justice. The dilemma is compounded by the failure of senior police officers to appreciate the work and worth of the subordinate staff and treat them with dignity and courtesy they deserve. I have witnessed noble human qualities in some of the officers working under me and felt inspired.

I have also conjured up memories of some of my old friends and associates, whose company enriched my life and gave me undiluted joy and happiness. Some of them have left us forever but their memories remain etched in my mind. Like Wordsworth's daffodils, in moments of solitude, they flash upon my inward eye. This retrospective glance on past events and recall of old memories has given me a sense of exaltation and also spurred self-introspection. I hope, the readers will find them of interest.

I convey sincere and appreciative thanks to my secretary Shri Rajib Kumar Majumdar for his constant help and valuable suggestions.

1
Malevolent Destiny

During my tenure as the Director of the National Police Academy, (NPA) Hyderabad, Surendra Nath, the then Governor of the Punjab, was a frequent visitor. Surendra Nath was an outstandingly successful officer of the Indian Police Service. In a glittering service career, spanning over four decades, he held many important offices with great distinction. Honour and recognition followed his footsteps. He was the youngest Inspector General of Police of the State of Jammu and Kashmir (J&K) and also the first IPS, Chief Secretary of Mizoram. Subsequently, he joined the Union Public Service Commission as a Member and later on became its Chairman. The climax of his long professional career was his appointment as the Governor of Punjab, at a time, when the State was convulsed by terrorist attacks and violence. He made a noteworthy contribution in the elimination of terrorist violence in the Punjab.

Surendra Nath often came to the NPA to address the IPS probationers. He was charming, urbane and silver-tongued. He always felt that the young IPS probationers, the police leaders of tomorrow, should be infused with correct values and ideas. Future of the police service in the country hinges largely on professional and moral leadership provided by the IPS officers. He, and his charming wife, endeared themselves to all by their unfailing courtesy and graciousness. During interaction with the probationers, he always emphasized, by quoting apt incidents and examples from his long professional career, the practical wisdom of eschewing extra-legal methods and cultivating respect for human rights. I also sought his counsel in many matters and issues concerning police training in the country.

Unfortunately, while travelling by air from Chandigarh to a place in Himachal Pradesh, he died alongwith all members of his family in a plane crash. It was a cruel stroke of malevolent destiny. It was a horrific and shattering blow to all of us, who knew, loved and admired him. Both my wife and I were left benumbed by shock and sorrow. I quoted to Gouri, the memorable lines of the Greek historian Herodotus "*Call no man happy until you hear the end of him*". I also recalled the poignant lines of AESOP describing the tragic elements of life. *The joys in life*, he says "*are the beautiful things in nature, the earth, the sun, the stars, the wheeling of the moon and the sun*". But *so far the* rest, there are fears and sorrows and "if one enjoys a little happiness, nemesis, exacts recompense".

After demitting charge as the Director of the National Police Academy, I joined as the Director General of the newly created National Human Rights Commission. This happened just before the tragic denouement. I received a posthumous letter from Surendra Nath dated 15th June, 1994, in which he congratulated me and wished all success in my new assignment. He said somewhat very generously "*it was a deserving recognition of your outstanding merit and qualities of character*". I had tears in my eyes.

Even now, after more than two decades, whenever I recall my days in the National Police Academy, Hyderabad, the smart and trim figure of Surendra Nath, with his ever-smiling face and brisk movements flashes before my mind's eyes. One cannot indeed fathom the mysterious ways of providence. A cruel stroke of malignant fate ended a bright and inspiring career of a stalwart of the Indian Police Service. But memories of association with him remain undimmed and imperishable.

2

An Ideal Trainer

Most of the police training institutions all over the country today are in a poor state of health. Besides inadequacies of infrastructural facilities, they have become dumping grounds of inefficient and often discredited officers and men, who command little respect from the trainees. Many of them instead of motivating the trainees, spread the message of frustration and cynicism. However, there are some refreshing exceptions — some titans among the minnows. One such was E.L. Stracey, who was Deputy Commandant of the Central Police Training College (CPTC), Mount Abu, where we had undergone our police training after joining the Indian Police Service.

CPTC was a make-shift institution hurriedly set up after independence. Training facilities were inadequate, if not poor. In the training curriculum, there was overemphasis on drill, parade, horse riding and physical exercises. To many probationers, CPTC was indeed an acronym for Constant Physical Torture College. Many of the trainers in both indoor and outdoor sections were inadequately equipped to train IPS officers and many suffered from various limitations and complexes.

But one person, who stood tall and commanded respect and awe, was the then Deputy Commandant E.L. Stracey, an IP officer from Tamil Nadu cadre. Smart, handsome and ramrod- straight, Stracey was an inspiring model; one of those ideal trainers, who took joy in imparting training to the budding leaders of the Indian Police Service. He took this training assignment with almost a missionary zeal and imparted to it some rare grace and flavour.

Stracey was a stickler for correct etiquettes and manners and took great pains in teaching the raw probationers how to hold correctly forks and knives at the dinner table, how to greet a lady and how to salute smartly in uniform. We used to call E.L. Stracey as *Etiquette Loving Stracey*. He could be stiff and blunt at times, but always sought to inculcate among the probationers, officer-like qualities. He had an eagle-eye and was quick to detect the lapses of the probationers at the parade ground and malapropisms in the class room. He would teach us how to salute properly and how to conduct ourselves befittingly on and off the parade ground. Colour of the socks not matching the shoes and trousers, hastily shaven cheeks and loose tie knots will not escape his eyes. We learned from him many a social grace and nicety. Though punctilious, he was never a heartless martinet. Behind the apparently tough exterior, there was warmth and concern for the well-being of the trainees. Once he noticed that one of the probationers was lowering his head too much while taking soup, he advised him not to do so and humorously added that horses do like that.

He used to take classes on police administration. He was not very sound on rules and procedures of police manuals or sections of the Indian Penal Code, but clear on fundamental ethical issues concerning policing. He always emphasized that short-cut extra-legal methods are impermissible and counterproductive and sully the image of the police, hampering good and efficient policing. After nearly four decades, when I had the privilege to join as the

Director of the National Police Academy, Hyderabad, Stracey was my inspiring role model.

At the entrance of the National Police Academy's office building on a black piece of marble the following lines are inscribed:

> "Michelangelo was once asked, "How do you produce statues that are so full of life"? Michelangelo said, "It is just a matter of extracting them. The rough marble already contains the statue. There is already a fine officer in you. Help us to chisel it."

Whenever, my eyes fall on those lines inscribed on the marble I think of Stracey. We heard from Stracey the vicissitudes of his service career and the sea of troubles he faced for not being a pliant officer. But ultimately, he reached the summit of police profession as the Director General of Police, Tamilnadu. He has narrated in his book, "*Odd Man Out in Indian Police*", the high and low watermarks in his service career, the difficulties he encountered for crossing swords with the politicians. He narrates all this with no sense of rancour.

So far work is concerned he would not spare anyone but would not pursue. Streaks of sadism and vindictiveness, which we have witnessed in many senior officers were conspicuously absent in him. He would tick off not only the probationers but also the instructional staff and even the senior officers coming for training in advance courses. He pulled up a senior officer (who, later on became a Member of the Parliament) for coming late as a player in the cricket field and for setting up a bad example before the junior officers and chastised senior outdoor trainers for using swear words in the parade ground. However, he also made it clear that the IPS probationers would have to follow the discipline of the parade ground and unquestioningly obey the directions of the field trainers. Once admonishing some errant probationers, he said that sometimes we have to be cruel in order to be kind. Firmness and fairness should go side by side.

Our training in Mount Abu also included a programme of *Bharat Darshan* to enable us to catch fleeting glimpses of the different parts of the country and understand its bewildering diversities and the underlying thread of unity. Our *Bharat Darshan* programme included a visit to Delhi and calling on the Home Minister Pandit Govinda Bhallav Pant. A stalwart of the freedom struggle, Pant was a venerable and powerful leader, enjoying a position only second to Nehru in the Central Government. During the interaction session, Pantji with his shaking hands (an after-effect of the blows received in a lathi-charge by the police during the British rule) expounded to us the new role of police in independent India. In the course of the discussion, Stracey raised before him the question that political masters want quick results against crime and criminals and, thus, indirectly pressure the police to adopt short-cut and quick-fix methods. Pantji, however, misunderstood the burden of this valid poser. He upbraided Stracey and called him an officer of the old school. The meeting ended in a sour note. We came out sadder but not wiser.

Nearly twenty years later, when I was serving as a DIG Western Range at Rourkela, I received a letter from MIS Iyer, the then Dy. Director of the National Police Academy mentioning that Stracey's sword would be kept in the Central IPS Mess. He asked me to suggest some appropriate lines to be inscribed in the brass below the sword. I wrote to Iyer that Stracey has become a living legend and will occupy a place of honour in the annals of the Indian Police Service. I suggested the following lines of Shakespeare to be inscribed on the brass below the sword :

> "Be just and fear not. Let all the ends thou aimst at be thy country's, thy God's and truths"

I sent a copy of the letter to Stracey, who was then Director General of Police, Tamilnadu. Stracey wrote back that "the compliments you pay are very touching; all the more because they are sincere. I only hope I deserve them".

I shall always recollect Stracey as the role model of a trainer. His handsome appearance, dignified bearing, graceful movements, eye for details, total commitment for training and unremitting endeavour to improve an institution set him apart as an ideal head of a training college. Today, many of the police training institutions are in a bad shape and some of them are just crumbling. We need outstanding committed officers like Stracey to head these institutions and impart to their dry bones, the Promethean spark of life. Unfortunately, many of these institutions are headed by people, who are singularly unfit for the job and only mark their time and think of shifting to greener and more lucrative pastures.

3
Empowering the Subordinates

The National Human Rights Commission came into existence in October, 1993. It was a landmark in the annals of human rights movement in the country. A blue ribbon Commission headed by a former Chief Justice of the Supreme Court was set up by the Government of India for protection and promotion of human rights in the country. The Protection of Human Rights Act 1993, armed it with adequate power and authority to enquire into cases of violation of human rights and recommend corrective measures.

Vigorous investigation and interventions by the Commission in high-profile cases captured public imagination and received wide coverage both in the print and electronic media. Not unexpectedly, the Commission was deluged with complaints of human rights violations from all over the country, including, abuse and misuse of authority by police and prison officials. As the Director General of Police in charge of Investigation, I had to take up investigation of many cases ordered by the Commission. The first Chairman of the Commission was Justice Ranganath Mishra, former Chief Justice of India. He was also the former Chief Justice of Orissa High Court. Handsome, fair complexioned with sharp aquiline features, Mishra looked every inch a judge. He spoke in a soft voice and measured every word carefully. Orders passed by him were clear and crisp and revealed a practical, cogent and organized mind. When greatly provoked by colleagues and errant subordinates, he would occasionally flare up but quickly regain his composure. He was also an excellent team leader and had the sterling capacity of carrying a heterogeneous group with him. In the meetings of the Commissions, sometimes sparks would fly. There were ego hassles. However, Mishra knew how to apply the healing balm and successfully assuage bruised feelings. Mishra knew the art of empowering his officers, repose trust in them and extract the best out of them. It was a joy to work with him. His familiar refrain was work with a smile on the face. He had an excellent equation with the then Prime Minister, and this helped the Commission to overcome quickly its teething troubles and get a flying start.

Despite his long judicial background, he was a man in a hurry and never allowed himself to be snowed under rules and procedures. In a petition received from an inmate in Tihar prison regarding torture and maladministration, he issued directive to call a meeting of the Home Secretaries and Inspector Generals of Prisons of differents states to examine various issues concerning prison administration leading to violation of human rights. NHRC's prestige at that time was at its apogee. There was immediate and overwhelming response from the States. Most of the States agreed to send their officers for this meeting convened by the NHRC. Myself, and Secretary General of the Commission R.V. Pillai, burnt midnight oil to prepare background papers and agenda for the conference. As the investigation wing was looking after human rights violations in prisons, it was primarily my job to sweat and to do the ground work. I was the prima donna. In the inaugural session, I outlined the objectives and structure of the conference and then requested Justice Mishra to deliver the key-note address. Justice's Mishra's address was clear and pithy. He explained the rationale behind the meeting and the overarching need for safeguarding the rights of men and women behind the prison walls. He feelingly referred to mounting incidence of deaths in jail custody and appalling and dehumanizing conditions prevailing in many prisons. In the plenary session that commenced after inauguration, I requested him or any other member of NHRC to chair the session. But to my surprise and bewilderment, he asked me to chair the session and came down from the podium with other NHRC members and sat with the participants. I was stunned by this totally unexpected development. With some trepidation, I took up the gavel and commenced the job. Some NHRC members, even the Secretary General, were not exactly very happy, with Justice Mishra's delegation of this responsibility to me. But in view of his categorical stand, they had to toe the line. He also remained present in the conference for some time as a gesture of encouragement to me. He was happy to note that I was able to live up to the responsibilities thrust upon me.

A decade and half has rolled by. I still vividly recollect the events of that day. It was the grand old man's unique way of encouraging and empowering the junior officers. It was another way of telling me that he appreciated my work in the Commission. In our seniority-bound, hierarchical administration, this kind of imaginative gesture is unbelievable. Our bosses in police and administration trapped in brief authority strut and fret upon the stage and never learn the gracious art of delegation. Only good leaders can think of such imaginative gestures to electrify the subordinates and win their undying loyalty.

4
Sunlight is the Best Disinfectant

"*Sunlight is the best disinfectant*" was one of the frequent sayings of Justice M.N. Venkatachaliah, former Chief Justice of India and former Chairperson of National Human Rights Commission (NHRC). He was the second Chairperson of NHRC. Under Justice Ranganath Mishra, the first Chairperson, the Commission had a flying start. It made its presence felt and expanded its activities in diverse directions. It could also live down the criticisms of many in the civil society that it was a "*Sarkari Commission*", created by the government to whitewash its omissions and commissions in the field of human rights.

Venkatachaliah was an eminent jurist and a man of great learning. His areas of interest encompassed law, religion, history and philosophy. But he was just not a dry and detached scholar, but a warm and friendly soul with passionate concern for human rights. Mishra gave a dynamic thrust to the multi-pronged activities of the Commission, Venkatachaliah tried to systematize and streamline its functioning. He was a great believer in methods and systems and often used to say "*God is in details*".

He enhanced the stature of the Commission by instilling into it a high moral authority and integrity. He used to tell me that the investigation division of the Commission, which I was heading at that time, must relentlessly expose misconduct and violation of human rights by the police and other government agencies, but the work and conduct of the investigating officers must be scrupulously fair and above board. Policing the police has to be done in a fair and transparent manner and rights of the police officers cannot be trampled on. As head of the investigation wing, my responsibility was to lead by example. He appreciated some successful investigation of custodial torture and redressal of grievances of the victims by our officers. He insisted on surprise visits to prisons and lockups to preclude the scope for cover ups and window dressing. When the International Committee of Red Cross (ICRC) wanted to visit prisons and detention centres of Jammu and Kashmir, the Union Home Ministry expressed reservations and feared that these visits might turn out to be intrusive and expose the country to international scrutiny and opprobrium. The NHRC, however, was able to persuade the government to permit these visits. Indeed, this transparent approach helped ICRC to visit prisons and detention centre in Jammu and Kashmir. This furthered the cause of human rights and silenced unsubstantiated criticisms.

Justice Venkatachaliah robustly upheld the independence and integrity of the Commission. NHRC was repeatedly urging the government to accede to the UN Convention against Torture 1987. The Ministry of Home Affairs informed the Commission that the question of India becoming a signatory to the Convention was discussed in Chief Ministers' conference in 1995 and majority of the Chief Ministers were found not in favour of India's accession to the Convention. In a powerful and well-argued memorandum to the government, Venkatachaliah argued that acceding to the Convention "*would signify to the world that we intend to conduct ourselves in a manner that we have decided ourselves to be in keeping with our most cherished values. This great country does not need to crouch behind the high wall of national sovereignty on the great issue of human rights*". India signed the Convention in June 1997 but it had not ratified the Convention. Before taking a decision to accede to the Convention, the then Prime Minister Deva Gowda was keen to meet the Chairman NHRC, but Venkatachaliah made it clear that it would not be in keeping with his position to go to the Prime Minister's office to meet him. They could either meet in the office of the Commission or any other convenient place. The meeting could not take place.

Venkatachaliah made fast disposal of complaints a priority area of concern. At his instance, the internationally well-known McKinsey and Company examined the problems affecting the grievance redressal function of the Commission. In a report titled "*Preparation for a Fresh Start*", it made a number of bold and innovative recommendations for quicker methods of disposal. Unfortunately, for a variety of reasons, the measures recommended by the McKinsey group to jumpstart the process could not be implemented. Increasing backlog of cases continues to haunt the Commission.

Venkatachaliah strongly felt that the Protection of Human Rights Act 1993, needed amendment. In order to enhance NHRC's administrative autonomy and credibility, he set up a seven-member advisory committee headed by the former Chief Justice of India A.H. Ahmedi to review the Act and suggest amendments. The Committee received notes and memoranda from the Chief Justices of various High Courts, Chairpersons of State Human Rights Commissions, Chiefs of Army, Navy and Air Force and various non-governmental organizations giving their views and suggestions to amend the Act. The Committee finalized its recommendations after an exhaustive deliberative process and gave it to the Commission in the form of a draft Amendment Bill to amend the main Act. However, the government, true to form, dragged its feet. The Amendment Act of 2006 ignored the salient recommendations of the Committee to improve the Commission's administrative autonomy, operational efficiency and institutional legitimacy.

Venkatachaliah was also a man of unblemished integrity. He set exemplary standards of probity and incorruptibility before his subordinates. Today, conduct of some of the judges and even Chief Justices of higher courts has sullied the image of the judiciary and shaken public confidence. Justice Venkatachaliah was like a knight "*sans peur et sans reproche*". In my long years of government service, I have never seen a person so keen to ensure that government funds are not misused or wasted. Any instance of careless extravagance would irk him beyond measure. When he joined as the Chairman of NHRC, he spurned proposals made by the establishment to renovate the office room and purchase slick office furniture and made clear that well-designed sturdy furniture could be obtained from the CPWD on payment of nominal hire charges. By his personal conduct he typified the maxim "*Noblesse Oblige*" rank imposes obligations. Unfailing courtesy and humility was another hallmark of his character. Whenever we visited him in his house, he would treat us with utmost civility and walk up to the gate to see us off. Will Durant has defined a gentleman as one "*who is perpetually considerate*". He was a gentleman to his fingertips. I think of his grace and courtesy whenever I accost bureaucrats and judges behaving with a stiff upper lip.

Many in the Commission used to complain that he was somewhat slow in taking decisions. He would pause, ponder and analyze before arriving at any conclusion. Sometimes, this delayed and stalled decision and slowed down the processes in the Commission, but because of his judicial background he felt that a decision taken in haste could turn out to be unfair and unjust. Even more than a decade after leaving NHRC, whenever I go to Bangalore, I meet the grand old man and draw inspirations from his ideas and ideals. I see him in his sunset glory. Like Wordsworth's "Skylark", he remains "*true to the kindred points of heaven and home*".

5

Essence of Law Enforcement

Law Enforcement and order maintenance is the prime responsibility of the police in any society. The word "Police" is derived from Latin word *Politia*, which stands for state or administration. Police is the main entity through which preservation of peace and order is ensured by the government. The job of the police is difficult, hazardous and can be incredibly thankless. Indeed, from no other profession, so much is demanded with so little recompense. Police profession also lionises toughness and machismo qualities, necessary for ceaseless battle against the forces of lawlessness and disorder.

This stern message was continuously drummed into our ears when we were I.P.S. probationers at the Central Police Training College, Mt. Abu. We were told that the police service was not for the weak and faint- hearted and not for people with namby-pamby thoughts and utopian ideas. The war against crime is unending, a sisyphean task, meant only for the tough and undaunted.

During my period of practical training as the Assistant Superintendent of Police, Cuttack, senior officers including my SP, repeated the same adage and asked me to forget what had been taught in the training school and adjust myself to the stark ground-realities. The dominant police view is that, *"ends justify the means"*, and for ensuring that criminals get their just deserts, the Police, if necessary, should bend rules and get round laws and not hesitate to practice what is called "noble cause corruption". Good policing is not possible by acting within the four corners of the law.

Fortunately, during that period, I have had the opportunity of coming in close contact with the then Chief Justice of Orissa High Court, R.L. Narasingham. He was a member of the Indian Civil Service (ICS) but opted for the judicial side. Short and slim with sparkling eyes and smiling face, he was a simple man unaffected by the majesty of the service he belonged to.

The first day I met him at the Cuttack club, his immediate question was why I never turned up at the tennis court a de-rigneur for an assistant superintendent of police. I mumbled some excuses, but there was no escape. Narsingham used to come regularly to play tennis in the club. I used to get calls from his Registrar that His Lordship wants me to come to the club to play tennis and that too in proper kit. Thus, Legan my initiation in tennis. The tennis marker of the club Pankaj gave me many useful tips and I was able to pick up the game tolerably well within a short spell. This proved to be a boon in my long service career. Later on, as the Director of the National Police Academy, I played and enjoyed tennis with the IPS probationers and thereby forged closer understanding with many of them.

However, to go back to my Cuttack days, I also had the chance of long and interesting tête-à-têtes with Justice Narasingham after the games. He had a sharp analytical mind and his observations on contemporary events and dramatis personae in Orissa's political firmament were both incisive and insightful. He also recounted with evident glee, interesting anecdotes, including, scandals about some of the leading lights of the club. Because of his civil service background, he was quick in taking decisions, a quality that many in the judicial fraternity lacked. I shall always remember one of his many memorable aphorisms which I have subsequently repeated to many of my junior colleagues and probationers. He asked me to always remember that the role of the police is to maintain law and order but order through law, otherwise, dacoits could any day maintain better order than the police.

Over the years, I came to understand and appreciate the importance and import of this insightful observation and tried to adhere to it to the best of my capacity. It helped me immensely in my discharge of duties. In police job, one has to constantly encounter the dregs of society, and witness man's inhumanity to man. Many policemen, says Berkley criminologist, Gordon Misner, "*picture themselves as crime fighters standing against the Mongol hordes without the support of the public, politicians or courts*". This misconceived zeal makes them imagine that the hardened criminals will not respond to normal methods of investigation and detection and so they resort to practices, which are downright questionable and illegal. But this, without doubt, is a perverted approach.

Crime is contagious, and there will be utter contempt for law if police themselves become lawbreakers. In any democratic society, law vests vast powers in the hands of the police to curb lawlessness of anti-social elements but also keeps provisions to ensure that these powers are not misused or abused to imperil the freedom of the citizens. The mandate of the police to use force to curb violence raises a fundamental issue that police themselves should not indulge in unnecessary or excessive use of force. A lawless police is an abomination in a free society. It is mistakenly argued that to control the dreaded criminals or terrorists, tough policing involving violation of laws and rules is necessary, if not unavoidable.

With my long years of experience in active policing, I have always felt that this is an erroneous argument, and there is always the danger of police officers sliding down the slippery slope. Once a certain degree of force is permitted, the police officers face an overwhelming temptation to apply as much force they consider necessary to obtain the sought-after information. I have seen promising careers of young police officers coming to a sad end on account of transgressing laws and perpetrating illegalities. They were driven by the mistaken notion that end justifies the means. In any conflict of ends and means, the point to be borne in mind is that if the ends are important enough to justify the means. Conviction of a criminal is important, but more important is the fact that in a liberal democracy, the police are expected to carry out their activities in a manner that enhances the values of a liberal society. Adoption of impermissible means may ultimately undermine the end. The Independent Commission of Police in Northern Ireland (Patten Commission) has aptly said that "bad application or promiscuous use of power to limit a person's human rights by such means as arrest, strip-and-search, house searches, can lead to bad police relations with the entire neighbourhood, thereby rendering in effect policing of those neighbourhoods impossible". Adoption of unlawful means damages the standing of the police and also its effectiveness. To my mind, Narasingham's perceptive words sum up the essence of law enforcement and order maintenance, indeed the core functions of the police.

6
A Fearless Judge

I first met Justice J.S. Verma in the room of the then Chairman of the National Human Rights Commission M.N. Venkatachaliah. Justice Verma and Justice Venkatachaliah were close friends with immense respect for each other. At Justice Venkatachaliah's request, he released my book on "*Human Rights in a Developing Society*" in a very well-attended function at the India International Centre. He analyzed beautifully the challenges before human rights in a developing society plagued by many contradictions and encouraged me with some appreciative comments on my work.

Justice Verma was a straightforward no-nonsense judge, who could be, when necessary, firm and very forthright. In the hawala case, better known as Vineet Narayan case, he caused a stir and ruffled many a feather of political executives, when he asked the CBI to investigate the case unfettered by extraneous pressures and report directly to the court. He evolved the doctrine of continuing mandamus. The collapse of the case at the trial stage because of shoddy investigation by the CBI and its failure to corroborate diary entries of payments of bribe to important personages left him dismayed. In many meetings with the police and CBI officers, he would often give vent to his anger and disappointment.

He succeeded Justice Venkatachaliah as the Chairman of the National Human Rights Commission. The two great judges, despite close bonds of friendship between them, were poles apart in many ways. Venkatachaliah was scholarly, philosophical and humane; Verma was, on the other hand, resolute, decisive and a little self-opinionated. But the two wonderfully complemented each other and were persons of unblemished integrity with unshakeable faith in human rights.

During Verma's tenure, the NHRC was active and vibrant and commanded respect as the doughty champion of human rights. The NHRC strongly castigated the Gujarat government for the communal carnage of 2002 and recommended CBI investigation into many cases of violence, rape and murder. The BJP governments, both at the centre and Gujarat, were miffed beyond measure but the unambiguous and courageous stand of the NHRC and Justice Verma enhanced the Commission's image and credibility as a robust defender of human rights. It was indeed, NHRC's finest hour. The NHRC's Gujarat enquiry also falsified the canards spread by interested elements that Justice Verma had pro-BJP and pro-Hindutva sympathies. It was a slanderous accusation. He was quintessentially a great and transparent judge — *sans peur et sans reproche*.

My tenure at the NHRC ended a few months after he joined, but I was in touch with him in connection with human rights training programmes of police officers and other law enforcement functionaries. The NHRC also sponsored a big-ticket research study on trafficking in women and children in India. It was conducted by the Institute of Social Sciences and I was its Chief Coordinator. The research study was nationally as well as internationally acclaimed.

During discussions in seminars and workshops, Justice Verma never used to mince words in expressing his frank views on men and events. He was strongly and unequivocally in favour of police reforms and would reiterate the view that for the success of good governance, the police should be as independent as the judiciary. He was always critical of central and State governments' unconcealed efforts to scuttle the directives of the Supreme Court on police reform. He used to allude to some outstanding police officers of high integrity known to him and say that he has not seen many in judicial fraternity living up to such high standards. He was also a stern critic of corruption and sloth and delay in judiciary and felt that some of the judges in High Court and Supreme Court by their acts and conduct are besmirching the image of the judiciary. He was strongly in favour of an All India judicial service so that bright young men and women are attracted to judicial careers.

During his tenure as the Chief Justice of India, the Supreme Court adopted a code of conduct for judges known as "Restoration of values of judicial life". Today, when the standards of probity of some of the judges of the apex court are being openly called into question by the civil society activists, there is not even a faint whisper against Justice Verma. He lived a simple and spartan life and never tried to earn money after retirement through arbitration and chamber practice.

A colleague of mine, who accompanied him during NHRC's visit to Gujarat after the gory communal riots of 2002, was moved by his abiding concern and compassion for the victims of communal riots. The NHRC not only roundly condemned the State government's failure to prevent communal riots but also decried economic and social ghettoisation of the minority communities. His landmark Vishaka judgment spotlighted the issue of sexual harassment at the work place. Using international treaties and conventions that India has signed, he breathed a new life into the fundamental rights of women, which the Parliament had failed to do. Recently, the Parliament has passed the bill on sexual harassment for women at workplace without any discussion. The fitting culmination of Justice Verma's distinguished career is the report he and his committee produced on rape law amendments. This was a sequel to the horrific gang-rape of a young woman in a Delhi bus. The path-breaking report did not confine itself to the mere amendments of rape laws but gave a new dimension to the concept of women's rights and gender equality. It is a pity that many of the salient recommendations of the report still remain unaddressed by the law makers.

Justice Verma left us forever in a blaze of glory. He will be remembered by many, who admired his forthrightness and courage of convictions. The controversy regarding the nature of the award given to him posthumously by the Government of India is unfortunate and unseemly. He will always have an abiding place in the hearts of those, who knew and admired him.

7
God is in Details

During my tenure as Director General in the National Human Rights Commission, I have had the opportunity to work closely with judges of the Supreme Court and State High Courts as well as some well-known civil servants. Some of the judges were mediocrities, viewing posting in the NHRC as *sine cures*. There was one Chief Justice of a High Court, who took a policy decision not to work. But there were other distinguished Members, who took the job with missionary zeal and tried to make the Commission a vibrant institution. Some of them indeed made a signal contribution for promotion and protection of human rights in the country. One such member was Justice V.S. Malimath.

Justice Malimath, a former Chief Justice of Karnataka and Kerala High Court, joined the Commission a few months after it started functioning. Reputation of his razor-sharp intellect, capacity for going into details and taking quick and correct decisions had preceded him. Justice Ranganath Mishra was then the Chairman of the Commission. Justice Mishra and Malimath in many ways, complemented each other and gave vigorous thrusts to the many-sided activities of the fledgling Commission.

For many of us, those were the wondrous days. The new institution, belying prophesies of many a Cassandra, was making its presence felt and causing flutter in some dovecots. By vigorously championing the cause of human rights, the NHRC instilled hopes and confidence in the minds of many forgotten and benighted souls. The Commission took up causes like Police reforms, repeal of draconian legislation like the TADA, which made the then government very uncomfortable.

Justice Malimath typified the quintessence of human rights and never displayed the pomp and aura of the high offices he once held. In his new incarnation as a Member of the Commission, he did not carry any baggage of the past. In my long career in law enforcement, I have seen many judges stuck in the time-wrap, not adjusting themselves to ground realities and remaining prisoners of the past. Malimath used to say that as a member of the Commission, his first task was to forget that he was once the Chief Justice of a High Court.

In the Commission, we have had moments of agony and ecstasy. In hours of stress and strain, we always used to turn to Justice Malimath for sage counsel and guidance. He offered healing touches and gave sound and pragmatic suggestions. He appreciated the work of the investigation wing of the Commission and my leadership role in building up a competent investigation team. The Commission, in its initial years, was deluged with complaints of human rights violations by the police. Many members of the Commission were uninhibited in their criticisms of the boorishness and malfeasance of the police. Some of the criticisms were well-founded and justified. But justice Malimath, while frowning on police misconduct and transgressions, also tried to appreciate the practical constraints of the police and the multitudinous duties they are called upon to perform. He was an unwavering champion of structural reforms of the police with a view to insulating it from external pressures and influence.

In the Commission meetings, his sound knowledge of law and clear and cogent reasoning impressed everyone. He had a great capacity to go into details. To him God was in details. In seminars and conferences, everyone appreciated his blazing intellect and ability to go into the heart of a matter quickly. Thus, in all such conferences, he was a big draw.

After demitting office as the Member of the Commission, Justice Malimath headed a Committee appointed by the Government of India on Reforms of the Criminal Justice System. The Committee viewed holistically the impediments and bottlenecks clogging the criminal justice delivery system of the country. The report contained many useful and practical suggestions for reinvigorating and streamlining the criminal justice system, now teetering on the verge of collapse. At his instance, I prepared a note for the Committee on Investigation and Prosecution, which he appreciated very much.

However, the Committee's Report invited criticisms from the legal purists because it recommended some bold and unorthodox measures to galvanize the system. I strongly feel that when the embers of controversies die down, the jurists and hyper-critical human rights activists will appreciate the practical recommendations embodied in the report. The report also reflects his abiding concern for the plight of the victims in the criminal justice system. Victims, as he often used to say, are forgotten in the Anglo-Saxon adversarial system and their grievances are as much with the procedure of the criminal justice system as with the supposed injustice of the outcome.

Another point, he often used to emphasize, during discussions and deliberations was that human rights have to be correlated to duties. The rights are unlikely to be abused if explained in terms of duties. He often quoted the well-known saying of Mahatma Gandhi "*I learnt from my illiterate but wise mother that all rights to be deserved and preserved must come from duty well-done. Thus, the very right to live accrues to us when we do the duty of citizenship of the world".*

Justice Malimath has now settled down in Bangalore and is functioning as the Chairman, Law Commission of Karnataka. Age has not dimmed his intellect nor withered his commitment to human rights issues. His infectious enthusiasm inspires me whenever I meet him.

8

Honour Lies in Acting One's Part Well

The Central Police Training College (CPTC) in Mount Abu was the training institution for officers of the Indian Police Service in 1950s and 1960s. Training was tough and backbreaking and there was an overwhelming emphasis on drill, parade, horse riding and physical exercises. The underlying assumption behind the rigorous regime was that IPS officers, who would assume leadership positions in the Indian Police would have to be like Spartan generals, tough strong and muscular to command respect and allegiance of the subordinates and firmly control criminals and anti-social elements. To many raw young IPS probationers, training in the CPTC, was a harrowing and agonizing experience. Coming out of the cloisters of the colleges and the universities, they were shaken by the abrupt and dramatic change of the environment and at a loss to adjust themselves to the tough and toilsome rigours of police training. They were constantly reminded that police service was not for the weak and faint-hearted. Some even thought of throwing in the towel and resigning. Consequently, probationers, deficient in parade and riding, were the butts of acid comments and sharp admonitions. Many in the CPTC Cassandra-like predicted that they would be totally unfit in police — square pegs in round holes.

The chief drill inspector in our days was Mr. S. Spadigam. He was from the Malabar Special Police and came on promotion to CPTC in the rank of the Deputy Superintendent of Police. Short, well built, swarthy with curly hair, he was a terror in the parade ground and used to roar at us whenever any lapses came to his notice. He had eagle eyes and could detect mistakes and even minor lapses of the probationers in the parade ground even from far distance. He had a repertoire of stinging words and phrases and made lavish use of them without discrimination while reproving us in the parade ground. Some of his comments were biting and also worth quoting. While ticking off a probationer in the parade ground for poor drill performance, he said that at the time of the drill test, the hapless probationer would have to swallow his own saliva. However, he was also keen to see that trainees, who were deficient in drill and parade improve their performance and catch up with others. I still recollect some of his acid comments like "You crooked specimens of humanity don't stand like dried brinjals". Again while reprimanding a probationer for his lacklustre performance in the parade ground, he advised him to die and assured him of a good police funeral. He was cut to the quick when he felt that IPS officers were not seriously trying to overcome their inadequacies and feared that they would become butts of disparaging comments of the subordinates when they would be posted in the field. He would take serious umbrage at any sign of indiscipline or sloppiness of the trainees because he genuinely felt that poorly-trained, ill-equipped and indisciplined officers would not be able to command men under them. While upbraiding some of us once he said that the young IPS officers are the police leaders of tomorrow; they have to command large bodies of men but their subordinates would not listen to them if they are lacking in the qualities of leadership. They must carry themselves with becoming dignity. But the dreaded martinet would totally change outside the parade ground. He would be genial, extremely affable and civilized and treat us with unfailing courtesy and consideration. It was like a caterpillar becoming a butterfly.

During our training days at CPTC many of us chafed at overstress on drill and parade which drained out our energy and made us sleepy in the indoor classes. But now with the wisdom of hindsight, I feel that parade and drill serve an important purpose. They ensure automatic coordination and discipline. Parade is derived from the Latin word "Parad" which means to set a place in order. There is need for physical fitness and stamina to withstand the rigorous requirements of the police job in the field. Spadigam truly believed that training should generate among officers a life-long obsession for physical fitness, a trait, which unfortunately many police officers do not possess.

Spadigam was just not a rough-hewn Police officer. He was well-read, and particularly well versed in English literature. He could quote "appropriate lines from Coleridge's Rhyme of the Ancient Mariner or Gray's Elegy. He once quoted lines from Tennyson's immortal poem 'The Charge of the Light Brigade' to highlight the need for defiance in defeat. He carried himself with dignity. Though a fairly junior officer in Police hierarchy, he was never sycophantic before senior officers. During discussions also, he would put across his point of view without equivocation. Probationers, as well as other outdoor trainers, feared but respected him and this respect he had earned by his total commitment to his job and compelling personality. He showed us that honour lies not from any condition but in acting one's part well.

Even now, when I recollect our days in Police Training College Mount Abu, the well-built swarthy figure of Spadigam strutting across the parade ground and fuming at the awe-struck probationers flashes before my mind's eye. Generations of IPS officers of our times will remember this human volcano with an ice-cap.

9

K. F. Rustamji

A Police Titan

K. F. Rustamji unarguably remains one of the Titans of the Indian Police. His vision, charismatic qualities of leadership, dignity and grace have inspired countless officers and men, who came in contact with him. In my long police career, I did not have the opportunity to work under him, but I met and interacted with him on different occasions. It was always an inspiring experience. In my early days in service, I was a frequent presenter of papers in All India Police Science Congress sessions. Rustamji on a few occasions chaired some of the sessions. I was invariably impressed by his superb articulation and capacity to go into the heart of a matter quickly and effortlessly. His observations were succinct and pithy and never strident. He also never allowed discussions to go off the rails.

In the early 70s, when I came to Delhi to join the Intelligence Bureau, Rustamji was heading the Border Security Force, which under his stewardship witnessed phenomenal expansion as well as consolidation. BSF officers revered him and would recount many incidents of his exceptional man management skill and capacity to see details with one eye and visions with the other. He was both a galley slave and a dreamer.

The role of BSF in the liberation war in Bangladesh is a part of history and Rustamji as the head of the force provided dynamic and sagacious leadership in those tumultuous days. Indeed, according to some discerning ringside observers, the liberation of Bangladesh would have taken a longer period if Rustamji had not been in overall charge of BSF operations. I had requested him on a few occasions to write about the panorama of stirring events of those days as they would have lighted up many unknown twists and turns of Bangladesh war and would have been of great historical interest, but Rustamji did not agree and said that he would "*take them to his grave*".

Rustamji was a member of National Police Commission (NPC) set up in 1978 after the Emergency. I recollect that some of us in a delegation on behalf of the IPS Association called on the members of the NPC to express our views on the imperatives of police reforms. Rustamji asked some very pertinent questions. NPC report, a landmark in the annals of Indian police, bears stamp of Rustamji's perspicacious thinking on different police issues.

When I was posted as IG and later on Addl. DG BSF in Kolkata, I would marvel at Rustamji's vision and capacity to take big and bold decisions and get them implemented. He was a starter as well as a sticker, a quality missing in many officers, and exuded infectious commitment and enthusiasm. He was, to quote the lines of Milton one of the

> "tall men, sun crowned, who live above the fog in public duty and in private thinking".

After joining as the Director of the National Police Academy Hyderabad, it was my privilege to invite him on many occasions to address the IPS probationers. He used to come and captivate the young bright officers with superb narration of many cases drawn from the reservoir of his vast experience and exposition of the ethical dimensions of policing. After my innings in the National Police Academy, I joined as the Director General of the National Human Rights Commission. I used to write articles on human rights issues in different papers and journals. Whenever any article of mine appeared in the press, I used to get an encouraging note from him. He himself was by then a respected columnist writing on policing, law enforcement and many other issues and educating the public of the hazards of poor governance. On one occasion, the NHRC was examining the untold public inconvenience caused by excessive and obtrusive VIP security arrangements. The Commission requested Rustamji to come and enlighten it with his expert views on the subject. The then Director Intelligence Bureau and GC Dutt, former, Chief Security Officer of the Prime Minister, were the two other experts invited by the Commission. Rustamji's views reflected his modern mind and he offered some pragmatic suggestions. The then Chairman of the National Human Rights Commission MN Venkatachaliah and other Members were very appreciative of his clear and uncluttered thinking on the subject.

After superannuation, Rustamji retired to Mumbai. On a number of occasions, I called on him in his flat at Peddar Road. As always, he was a picture of grace and dignity. With keen and alert mind he would ask many questions and offer his considered views on different subjects. During his service career, Rustamji bestrode like a colossus but I have always felt that, he was, as poet Rabindranath Tagore in a moving poem had written on Emperor Shahjahan "*greater than his deeds and truer than his surroundings*".

10

Remembering J.C. Ghosh

I still vividly remember my first meeting with J.C. Ghosh. It was sometime in March, 1962, when I was posted in Cuttack for training as a probationary Assistant Superintendent of Police along with another batchmate of mine P.K. Mishra. This was a part of our field training, when under the watchful eyes of an experienced Superintendent of Police we had to learn the nuts and bolts of police work in the district. It was drummed into our ears that this training regime, unless taken seriously, will make us ill-equipped and ill-prepared to shoulder important charges of district. Policing can be a tough and a risk-filled assignment because a serious mistake or omission at a critical juncture can jeopardize an officer's career and land him in a black hole. Learning by trial and error can prove to be a hazardous venture.

J.C. Ghosh, an IP officer, at that time, was the Inspector General of Police, Orissa. He was the senior-most officer of the police hierarchy of the State. The posts of Director General of Police or countless officers of same rank had not yet surfaced and the police hierarchy was far from being flabby or top-heavy. Ghosh hailed from a distinguished family from Bihar and was known for his unblemished probity. He was also, unlike many Indians in authority, a man of few words. It was *de-rigueur* that the Assistant Superintendent of Police must call on IG of police as early as possible. One morning, my friend P.K. Mishra and myself in full ceremonial dress, and perspiring profusely out of a sense of nervousness and trepidation, called on him in his office. We were advised by the Superintendent of Police to be careful and deferential and also to inform I.G. in no uncertain manner that SP was leaving no stone unturned for our proper training. When we marched into his room at Police headquarters, we found that Ghosh, a heavy middle-aged man with an impassive face and grim look, was pouring over some files. He raised his eyes from the files and had a close look at both of us. For next few minutes he did not utter a word and the two of us remained petrified in our chairs. I could, however, despite forbidding silence, notice a kindly humorous benign gleam in his eyes. After this brief (which at that time seemed unending) pause of silence, he made some queries regarding our training and asked us to go and meet the other senior officers in the office. We scampered out of his room a little dazed and unsure of the impression, IG had formed about us.

After a few months, my friend and batchmate P.K. Mishra got married. Mishra's marriage took place in his native place at Bolangir, but he arranged, after a few days, a tea party at the bungalow which we both were sharing at that time. The invitees were mostly senior officers of the service. Many of the senior officers did not care to turn up. Some came late and unblushingly offered some trite excuses. But the senior-most officer of the cadre, J.C. Ghosh along with his wife, came exactly in time and showed by personal example that the marriage ceremony of an ASP is an important function which senior officers should make it a point to attend in time.

Many other incidents and episodes associated with Ghosh flash before my mind's eyes. I never worked with him as one of his staff officers, but often had the opportunity of coming in close contact with him while I was posted in Cuttack. Behind his frosty exterior and apparent unapproachability, there was a kind and warm soul always eager to right the wrongs brought to his notice. I have also never seen him speaking disparagingly or pejoratively of others, who had always not been fair to him. Like Newman's "True gentleman" he had too much good sense to remember injuries and nurture grudges against others. Will Durant has defined gentleman as one who is "perpetually considerate". Ghosh was also invariably kind and considerate, qualities which are mistakenly considered as unpolice-like. Students of Greek history know that Brasidas, the noblest of Spartans, was called a Spartan by mistake. J.C. Ghosh was perhaps a police officer by mistake.

Once, with some of his friends he visited our house in Charbatia, a place near Cuttack, where I was then posted as the Commandant of the Orissa Military Police Battalion. He was at that time functioning as the Transport Controller. One of his friends, who was also known to me requested for a police tent to be used in a picnic, which they planned to organize in a nearby location. There were procedural difficulties in acceding to the request and so I kept mum. In the evening, I got a phone call from J.C. Ghosh from Cuttack. He felt that perhaps I was feeling inhibited to give a negative reply to his friends in his presence and advised me not to comply with the request as the police tentage cannot be given for the use of private individuals.

A senior civil servant is expected to be honest, but Ghosh's standard of integrity was perhaps one of the highest to be seen in a government officer. He set up highest standards of propriety and incorruptibility before his subordinates. There was not even a faint whisper against his character and conduct.

Ghosh was, however, slow in taking decisions. Though upright, he was not outspoken even when circumstances warranted. I remember a conference of senior police officers in Cuttack way back in 1962 when the then Chief Minister Biren Mitra spitefully railed against Orissa Police and its top leadership for various alleged omissions and commissions. Some of his observations were figments of imagination and not based on facts. He was maliciously briefed by some elements within the force who wanted to discredit Ghosh. It was an unbridled smear campaign. Many young officers like us were squirming in our chairs and wanted a forceful rebuttal from IG of Police. But Ghosh remained impassive and neither rebutted nor confronted the Chief Minister. Not faintheartedness, but his innate sense of dignity perhaps prevented him from an unseemly passage-at-arms with the Chief Minister. After gory communal riots at Rourkela in 1964, the government replaced him as IG of Police for failure to provide directions and leadership to the force and preventing communal riots that engulfed Rourkela. It was a trumped-up charge and subsequent enquiries vindicated Ghosh. When the new government came to power after the defeat of the Congress, Ghosh was rehabilitated and reposted as IG of Police. I have seen him in some of his moments of agony and ecstasy. He was never off balance and always retained a sense of poise and dignity.

Times are changing. The values of the old world we saw when we entered the service are being eroded and replaced by altogether new concepts and perceptions. J.C. Ghosh carried with him grace and aura of the old era. After retirement, he went to Calcutta, where he breathed his last. When I communicated the news of his death to one of my colleagues who just said, "Here comes the end of a good man". In this cruel and self seeking world around us, the number of truly good and civilized human beings is not many. The death of such a good man brings silent tears in the eyes of those, who knew and admired him. The saying of Socrates just before his death comes to one's mind "Think this certain, that to a good man no evil can happen in life or death". J.C. Ghosh was a good man.

11
Victim of Her Own Success

Kiran Bedi's decision to quit the Indian Police Service makes one sad. She is seeking retirement almost two years before her superannuation to devote herself, as she says, in academic pursuits and social causes. She feels that Indian Police Service no longer gives her any further sense of satisfaction and fulfilment. I have known and seen Kiran as a police officer for a more than two decades. She is a trailblazer — the first woman to join the Indian Police Service. In the sixties, when we joined the Indian Police Service the general belief was that the IPS is meant for tough and sturdy chaps willing to face many a hazard and not for the weaklings. It requires both brains and brawns. Certainly it was a *terra incognita* for young women. Kiran was the first to explode the myth and like a battering ram broke the wall of the male fortress. Later on many women officers joined the Indian Police Service and enriched it in many ways. As the Director of the National Police Academy, I have seen how young women probationers could outshine and outperform their male counterparts not only in indoor studies but also in outdoor games and exercises. Many of them afterwards blossomed as outstanding officers and added lustre to the service.

Kiran has always been dynamic and a go-getter. She raged

and raved against stultifying rules and procedures and never hesitated to express her views publicly, which sometimes landed her in controversies. Some of the senior officers have felt disturbed and discomfited because of her outspoken comments. However, the fact remains that in every charge she held, she left things a little better then she found them. Instead of only complaining against the system, she tried to improve things and usher in innovative changes. Her work as the Inspector General of Tihar Prisons has been truly outstanding. As the Director General of National Human Rights Commission, I had to often visit the Tihar Prison complex, and I have seen how she not only improved the physical infrastructure of the complex but also inspired and motivated the prison staff. One of the banes of the prison administration of the country is that the prison staff are for a variety of reasons demoralized and dispirited and not developed any pride in the profession, which is the key to excellence. Prison administration, thus, remains mired in attitudes and practices that are obsolete and antiquated. She was able to impart a new Promethean spark of life in the dry bones of Tihar prison administration. Indeed, everywhere she had worked she had been able to enthuse the subordinates and display inspirational qualities of leadership.

Today, the Indian Police and Administrative service have become totally politicized. Politicians rule the roost and the officers crawl when they are asked to bend. Someone has aptly said that crawling is always the best and safest as one cannot be knocked down from that horizontal position. Political masters are not comfortable with officers, who are not willing to do their bidding. Kiran is perhaps the only serving officer I know who has come out loud and clear in support of police reforms seeking to insulate the police from extraneous pressures and making it people's police and not the police of the ruling party.

However, like all mortals, she also has her foibles. There is criticism that she is a publicity hound and too often addresses the press in violation of service conduct rules. In a democratic society, the media has a mighty role in shaping and moulding public opinion, but too much glare of limelight can create problems for the public servants.

As the Director General of Bureau of Police Research and Development (BPR&D) she made her presence felt and galvanized the organization. She has not followed the beaten track and taken many new and bold initiatives, which will have far-reaching impact on the organization. I wish she had continued as the head of the BPR&D instead of quitting the service. BPR&D constitutes the think tank of the Indian Police and at this critical juncture, when the Indian Police is grappling with enormous challenges, BPR&D has a seminal role to play in planning, mapping and working road maps for the Indian Police. Kiran should have remained at its helm at this time.

It is a crowning pity that an outstanding officer like her, who has been a role model and inspired many young men and women to join the police service, is quitting with a sense of disillusionment. However, the decision to remain or quit the service rests with her. Here one should listen to the voice of the heart and take a decision according to one's own lights. Perhaps a new phase of her career with greater opportunities for serving the society will unfold. One wishes her best of luck. The Indian police will miss her.

12
Remembering Russi Mody

The news of the demise of versatile grand old man Russi Mody brings back to mind many old memories. I first met Russi Mody in his plush office at the Tata Iron & Steel Company (TISCO) at Jamshedpur. I was at that time posted at Jamshedpur as the Asst. Director of the Intelligence Bureau. Short, fair-complexioned with a cherubic face and flashy eyes, he was bubbling with energy and enthusiasm. He had just joined as the Managing Director of Tata Iron & Steel Company replacing R.S. Pandey, an IAS officer of Bihar cadre. Even in our first meeting, he spoke stridently and at length of corruption and mal-administration in the steel plant under his predecessor and made clear his plan to set things right by launching a cleansing campaign. He further said that corruption in any country or organization starts upstream and hence, he will first target some of the big fish. True to his word, he did this with a vengeance. Some of the senior officers of the steel plant were unceremoniously booted out and the clear message was sent that the new boss would not suffer people with questionable integrity. There were dark whispers that the cleansing drive was selective and people reportedly close to Pandey were shown the door. But I could learn from friends and other reliable sources that officers given marching orders were really persons of dubious integrity, who got their "*just deserts*".

During my tenure in Jamshedpur, I used to meet him off and on and discussed many issues and events. He was always gracious, but invariably frank and forthright in his opinions about prominent men and events in Bihar as well as in Delhi. He had a group of "Young Turks" loyal and close to him. These young acolytes were viewed as Carpet baggers by other TISCO officers and were subjects of vituperative, and, at times, malicious comments. I had occasions to interact with some of them and was impressed by their intelligence, gift of the gab and loyalty to Mody.

Mody, however, was very popular with the workers of Tata Steel Plant. They lionized him and looked up to him as their benevolent protector. Indeed, some of them were fanatically loyal to him. Though, at times, erratic and mercurial, he was always broad-minded and regal so far the TISCO workers and their family members were concerned. But because of his explosive temper and off the cuff abrupt remarks, he made quite a few enemies, who were spoiling to settle scores with him. He was not very popular with the district administration, though TISCO was bending backwards to cater to the various and, at times, unreasonable demands of the district administration. The then District Magistrate, perhaps, with the covert encouragement of the Chief Minister, wanted to twist his tail and harass him by framing some odd cases. There was no substance in them. Different wings of the district administration and State Intelligence Agencies collected reports about various omissions and commissions of Mody and the plan was to slap some criminal cases against him. I had to intervene and make clear to the district authorities, if this overtly malicious course of action is pursued, I shall have no other option but to report the whole matter to the

Intelligence Bureau and the Ministry of Home Affairs, exposing the shenanigans of the district administration. This perhaps was the clincher. Good sense prevailed on the district authorities and they desisted from this clumsy and vindictive exercise.

From Jamshedpur, I went on transfer to Delhi as the Deputy Inspector General of Police in the Shah Commission of Enquiry that was set up to probe into the excesses of the emergency, imposed by Indira Gandhi. Mody used to tell me of some of the gross excesses perpetrated by district administration during the emergency when citizens could not exercise their fundamental rights and the lamp of democracy had been snuffed out. As an industrialist, he was happy at the peace and order prevailing in the country but overwhelming concentration of power in one centre and consequent misuse of authority deeply distressed him. I heard from him how JRD Tata was forced to drop Nani Palkhiwala from some of the boards of Tata Companies because of extraneous pressures on him. Palkhiwala had become *persona non grata* because of his principled, courageous stand against the emergency.

After my innings in the Shah Commission, I went back to my parent Cadre in Orissa and was posted in Rourkela as the Western Range DIG. Keonjhar, a mining district, inhabited mainly by the tribal population, was in the Western range. During one of my visits to Keonjhar, I had gone to inspect the Police High School there. The school building was creaking and crumbling and there was no hostel for the wards of the police personnel, where they could stay and continue their studies uninterruptedly when the officers move out on transfer. The limited sum available with the District Welfare Fund was inadequate for the construction of a new hostel building.

TISCO had a number of iron mines in Keonjhar district and had maintained good relations with the district police. Drawing on my old friendship, I wrote a letter to Russi Mody seeking help from TISCO for construction of a hostel building. In my letter, I mentioned that the resources of the district police were limited and we would very much appreciate a generous gesture from TISCO. Response of Mody was prompt and gracious. He sent a cheque of rupees one lakh on behalf of TISCO. Never before TISCO had helped any institution of Orissa Police in this manner. In a "Thank-You" letter to Mody, I wrote that "*this gesture in keeping with the philanthropic traditions of TISCO, has been deeply appreciated by the district police personnel*". This was my last official contact with him.

Subsequently, I briefly met him on a few occasions either at airports or in some social functions. He had, by that time, fallen out of favour with Tata management and its helmsman Ratan Tata and was ploughing a lonely furrow. The old fire had gone but he remained alert and articulate as before and the light in his eyes flashed occasionally.

13

Forgotten Police Chief Shri S.K. Ghosh

I still recall my first meeting with him. We were then undergoing training at the State Police Training College at Angul in Orissa. On completion of I.P.S. training in the Central Police Training College at Mt. Abu, five Assistant Superintendents of Police of our batch in Orissa cadre joined the Police Training College (PTC) Angul. Training at Angul was meant to impart to the I.P.S. officers knowledge of State Police rules, regulations and local laws, and nitty-gritties of State police administration. Training facilities at P.T.C. Angul were inadequate, if not minimal. Our instructors were mostly Inspectors and Deputy Superintendents of Orissa Police. They were, despite limitations, courteous and knowledgeable and somewhat in awe of I.P.S. officers. In the past, some of the I.P.S. officers undergoing training did not behave with them with becoming courtesy and displayed snootiness which rankled some of them.

The Principal of the College at that time was Shyam Sunder Padhi, an I.P.S. officer of 1951 batch. He was by profession an engineer, who chose a police career and reached the top of the ladder. Padhi was then a bright strapping officer, full of beans, and bubbling with many novel and unorthodox ideas. He used to hold forth with great gusto, his views and ideas (somewhat unconventional) on the challenging nature of law enforcement and the role of I.P.S. officers in improving policing in the country.

One morning, he informed us in a hushed voice that the then-IG Vigilance of Orissa Police, S.K. Ghosh, on his way to Sambalpur, would break journey at Angul and interact with us. We heard stories, some true and some apocryphal, about S.K. Ghosh, a dynamic police officer, under whose charge the office of IG Vigilance had become a powerful and dreaded institution. We were asked to be deferential and careful in expressing our views before him.

Ghosh looked every inch a police officer, with cropped hair, agile movements and roving eyes. He was short, lean, wiry and squint-eyed. He burst upon us like a raging storm. Without much ado, he straightway told us that I.P.S. officers have to be honest and upright and, like Caesar's wife, must be above any taint of suspicion. There can be no compromise with sleaze and corruption of senior police officers. He mentioned about the case of one I.P.S. officer, who had been placed under suspension because of venal activities and vigilance enquiries set afoot against some other officers for criminal misdemeanour. He expressed the hope that we would turn out to be professionally competent and command respect of the subordinates by our professionalism. He further narrated with great gung-ho some of the unorthodox methods employed by him in handling law and order situations. His proclaimed *modus operandi* were at variance with what we had been taught at the Police academy. We were left dazed but also impressed with his single-minded commitment to curb corruption in the police.

After completion of training in Angul, I was posted in Cuttack as the Assistant Superintendent of Police. I used to call on Shri S.K. Ghosh now and again, and saw him a little more closely.

As the head of the Vigilance Department, he has made his presence felt all over the State administration by organizing raids detecting evasion of commercial taxes and launching prosecution against some venal public servants. He had an excellent equation with the then Chief Minister, Orissa, Shri Biren Mitra and the Chief Secretary, Shri Shivaraman. They supported him to the hilt and this support from the top made him a formidable and larger-than-life figure in bureaucratic circles. He had his acolytes in the Police who belauded him and critics who questioned his methods and felt that he was ruthless and vainglorious.

In 1964, Orissa witnessed gory communal riots at Rourkela, resulting in large-scale murder and mayhem of the minority community. The then-IG of Police, J.C. Ghosh, was given marching orders by the State government for his command failure. He was replaced by S.K. Ghosh as the new IG of Police. S.K. Ghosh was desperately keen to become head of the Police force and now his dream came true. As IG of Police, S.K. Ghosh showed his mettle and displayed initiative and enthusiasm of the highest order. Indeed it was his finest hour. With the support of the Chief Secretary and the Chief Minister, he brought about remarkable, all-round and unprecedented expansion of Orissa police and instilled in its dry bones a new spark of life. His presence was felt everywhere. When I was posted as the Superintendent of Police of Kalahandi, my first charge as the District SP, he summoned me and gave me useful advice and warnings before I went to assume my new charge. He asked me to study the District Gazetteers and keep myself informed of relevant facts and information concerning the district. He indeed took great interest in overseeing the work of the District Superintendents of Police and pulled them up whenever they were remiss. He came for a hurried inspection of Kalahandi Police District and the thing which impressed me most was that the inspection note of the District Police Office was issued by him on the same day. These days the inspection notes of senior officers are either not issued or issued after inordinate delay.

Life of S.K. Ghosh revolved round police and he thought, talked and dreamt about police all the time. There was a messianic zeal in him to expand and strengthen Orissa police and he was able to accomplish it within a brief span of time. Indeed, Orissa police witnessed a renaissance. But Ghosh, though personally incorruptible, had some serious flaws in his mental constitution. He was weak in ears and a man of very strong likes and dislikes. A colleague described him as "*a good friend but a dangerous enemy*". He would adopt means fair or foul to cut to size officers, who crossed his path. He sometimes failed to display magnanimity expected of a Chief. He had also a number of crony officers, who would poison his ears with stories of alleged misconduct of selected officers towards whom they were inimically disposed, and Ghosh would take serious notice of those motivated tittle tattles. This, created against him inveterate adversaries, who were biding their time and sharpening their knives to settle scores with him.

In 1967 election in Orissa, the Congress was defeated and a new coalition Government, led by R.N. Singh Deo, Raja of Bolangir, came to power. One of the first acts of the Government was to replace S.K. Ghosh and few other officers, who were considered to be closely aligned with the erstwhile Congress Government. Ghosh, however, did not remain in oblivion for a long time. The new Government wanted to make use of his professional expertise and brought him back as IG-Vigilance. But Ghosh remained unreconciled and felt that justice had not been done to him, by posting another officer junior to him in service, as IG of Police. He was bitter in his criticism of the new IG and constantly in a sulk. The Orissa police was cleft into two warring camps. Ghosh also aligned himself closely with one group of the coalition Government in power. The Chief Minister, a wily politician, bided his time and waited for an opportunity to outsmart and out-manoeuvre Ghosh. The propitious moment came when a Judicial Commission set up to enquire into sexual misconduct of an I.P.S. officer, recorded some adverse observations against Ghosh. The State Government seized this opportunity and compulsorily retired him from service, without a show-cause notice. It was a well-timed knock-out punch. Ghosh protested, raved, went to the court, but it was of no avail. All India Service Rules empowered the Government to take such course of action against an officer above the age of 50 years. This was an unexpected denouement, a tragic culmination of a career totally wedded to the cause of police. Even at the height of his power and authority, Ghosh did not self-aggrandize, and remained squeaky clean.

After the unceremonious exit, he settled in Calcutta and completely immersed himself in writing books on police subjects. He wrote a large number of books on different police topics and became a well-known figure in the world of police scholars. Academic pursuits provided the necessary anodyne and an appropriate channel to divert his boundless energies. He did not bemoan his lot with complaints and ailments and found Elysium in the world of books and studies. The books written by him, though not always very analytical, were rich in data and revealed his prodigious capacity for work and knack of going into details. Some of the books light up many dark corners of police profession. Once he told me, when I called on him at his Lake Town residence, that reading and writing books has provided him the ballast and enabled him to transcend personal sorrows and misfortunes.

Very few in Orissa Police now remember him. With inexorable passage of time, his many-sided contribution for expansion and efflorescence of Orissa police is forgotten. But any objective chronicler of Orissa Police's history will record with respect his undying commitment for and contribution to Orissa Police. Notwithstanding some flaws and foibles, he rendered yeoman service to Orissa police.

14

K.P.S. Gill

A Man of Steel

India's success in thwarting Khalistani terrorism in Punjab and bringing the State back from the brink of an abyss will always be linked with the name of a police officer of outstanding courage and ability. He is K.P.S. Gill. He is belauded in and outside the country for the dynamic and bold leadership he provided to the Punjab police in combating the scourge of terrorism. It was the worst of all times and many feared that Punjab convulsed by terrorist violence, murder and mayhem would break away from the country, and the accompanying flame of counter violence would tear asunder the country's federal structure.

Fortunately, the Punjab police at this testing time got as DGPs, two outstanding police leaders to lead the fight back against terrorist violence — Julio Ribeiro and K.P.S. Gill. Both were different in many ways but wonderfully complemented each other. Julio Ribeiro revived the flagging morale of the police and strengthened their resolve to fight back and not yield ground to foreign inspired terrorist goons. At that time, demoralization had set in the Punjab police and there was some infiltration of the terrorists in its ranks. Sections of the Hindu population in Punjab had started feeling that Punjab police was not non-partisan and clamoured for greater deployment of the central police forces like the CRPF and BSF.

K.P.S. Gill, who succeeded Ribeiro led the Punjab police from the front to deliver hammer blows to the terrorists. The situation was grim. It was indeed the time for, to quote the memorable words of Danton, "*audacity, more audacity and yet audacity*". Many faint-hearted officers, were leaving no stone unturned to avoid posting in Punjab. I know personally of an officer of the Indian Audit and Accounts Service (IAAS) going to the High Court to obtain an injunction against his posting order in Punjab by offering various specious pleas. It was indeed war 'a outrance' between the police and the terrorists armed to the teeth, flushed with funds and withdrawing when the heat was on to safe havens across the border. Gill resuscitated the drooping morale of the police. Tall, straight and taciturn, he knew the art of electrifying men under his charge and instilling in them a burning desire to fight back. When the terrorists, with a view to undermining and demoralizing the police officers, started to attack their houses and kill their near and dear ones, Gill's message to the force was to pay the cowards back in their own coins. Officers and men gallantly responded to his call and came forward to man the vulnerable posts savaged by the terrorists and settle scores with them.

There were criticisms from the civil society groups of Gill's unorthodox methods and lack of regard for human rights. Gill took all this in his stride. Once in my presence, he silenced a journalist critical of his strong-arm methods by saying that the fight between the police and khalistani terrorists was quintessentially a fight among the Jat Sikhs and others need not bother and interfere.

Before his embattled officers and men, he stood as a towering symbol of resolution and defiance. When as the Director of the National Police Academy, I invited him to take the salute in the passing out parade of the IPS probationers, many eyebrows were raised. Some *status* quoists were not happy because instead of calling political dignitaries like the President of India, Prime Minister or the Home Minister, as was the prevailing practice, I called a serving police officer to do the honours. But I felt that this would be an appropriate recognition on our part of the yeoman service he had rendered at a critical juncture in country's history. The probationers were elated and excited and Gill rose to the occasion and gave a stirring call to the young police leaders to be catholic and secular and fight to the last to uphold the country's honour and the best traditions of the Indian police.

His heroic service to the nation outweighs the plaintive criticisms. It is true that Punjab Police's battle against terrorism had been one of the most lethal of all counter-terrorist campaigns in the world. It was indeed a war-like situation. And during this high noon of terrorism in Punjab, there were some avoidable excesses by the police. Some wounds still remain unhealed and rankle the victims. Some of the omissions were *bona fide*, but few were deliberate. Supervisory authorities in and outside the police like the magistracy failed to exercise proper supervision to prevent abuse of untrammelled authority. This is a criticism that as head of the force Gill cannot escape.

One feels sad that Gill did not get appropriate recognition from the country's political masters, when the hydra-headed monster of terrorism was vanquished in Punjab and peace dawned after a long nightmare. Some of his unorthodox methods have got wider publicity than his achievements and service to the nation. Some of his omissions were trumpeted and achievements went unheralded. There was an orchestrated campaign to belittle him. Gill, however, stands out through the miasma of spite and rancour as one of the most towering police leaders of our times. He enjoys an abiding place of honour in the hearts of many all over the country.

15
Hidden Tears

Mrutunjay Tripathy was a well-known and well-acclaimed officer of Orissa police. After joining the Indian Police Service and completion of training at Central Police Training College, Mt. Abu, I was posted as the Assistant Superintendent of Police, Cuttack. Mrutunjay Tripathy, better known to his colleagues and subordinates as Mrutunjay Babu, was holding the office of the Superintendent of Police, Criminal Investigation Department, (CID) at that time. He was respected by all and one for his professional competence and unblemished integrity. He joined the Orissa Police in the rank of a Sub-Inspector, but soon made his mark because of his unquestioned integrity and outstanding investigative skill. He had, in his career as a police investigator; unravelled many complicated cases and justly won the reputation of being an ace-Investigator of Orissa police. Because of his sound professional competence, the subordinates were mightily scared of him. They knew that they would not be able to pull wool over his eyes. He would quickly detect their tricks and designs and come down on them like a ton of bricks. He himself was not only honest but would never blink at the shenanigans of the subordinates. This was unlike many so-called honest public servants, who despite their personal rectitude, would never dare to disturb the hornet's nest because of the fear of getting stung.

At that time in Orissa Police, the scope of promotion of officers from ranks was limited and senior posts were few. Mrutunjay Babu, however, was one of the few from the ranks to be promoted and given an important responsible charge. As Superintendent of Police (CID), he used to scrutinize carefully the supervision notes of important criminal cases by senior police officers and offer critical comments regarding the line and loopholes in the investigation of cases. With the erosion of police professionalism, this important role of State CID is now being relegated to the background. At that time, we were all scared of the acid comments on our supervision notes that would come from the Crime Branch.

Short and somewhat rotund, Tripathy was a man of few words. Occasionally, I used to drop in his office to seek his advice in case-related matters. I knew that a monstrous tragedy darkened the life of this dedicated and upright officer. His two sons had become convicted criminals. Stories were circulating about the dark deeds of his sons and exposed Tripathy to malicious gossips and ridicule. There were cluckings of tongues and dark innuendos about Tripathy's failure to rear up his children properly. Tripathy bore this tragic misfortune with unruffled equanimity.

One day, I ventured to ask him as to how this catastrophe happened to a man of his unquestioned probity. He slowly unburdened himself and narrated a poignant tale which wrenches my soul even today. He said that he started his career as a Sub Inspector of Police and went up the ladder by dint of hard work. The work of a Sub Inspector in charge of a police station is strenuous, unbelievably thankless and full of snake-pits. He remained scrupulously honest but because of the relentless pressure of work could not look after the upbringing and education of his sons. The youngsters came in touch with the bad characters coming and going out of police stations or locked in police hazats and developed criminal propensities. He was often out of the police station for days in the investigation of cases. His illiterate wife could not exercise any brake or control over the young sons going wayward. It was like sliding down the slippery slope, and once it started, there was no return.

I heard the doleful tale in stunned silence. There was a big lump on my throat and my eyes were moist. In my long career in the police, I am privy to the problems of police officers and the toll the police job takes on them. With pressure of work sometimes, over sixteen to seventeen hours a day, unhygienic surroundings and limited or almost non-existent facilities for rest and recuperation, the health of many officers get shattered and many descend into paths of depravity and suffer from benighted family life. But the fate of an uncompromisingly honest officer like Tripathy and pathos of his life fills one with a deep sense of sorrow. The eternal question as to why providence inflicts such terrible sufferings on right-minded people remains unresolved and unanswered.

16

In Memoriam

I first met Bishwapriya when I was a third-year student in Presidency College, Kolkata. It was a chance encounter at India Coffee House, located in a building formerly known as Albert Hall adjacent to the Presidency College. In those days, for young Presidency College students, the siren song of the Coffee House was irresistible. Sipping coffee and munching nuts, we chatted for hours and passed judgments over everything under the sun. Discussions ranged from interesting or boring lectures of the college professors to the fleeting charm and smile of the pretty girls of different classes.

In the fifties, Calcutta was a beautiful city with a charm of its own and the Presidency College had a magical atmosphere built up by learned and committed professors and bright students. Indeed, blessed it was to be alive in that dawn. We also betrayed an unwarranted intellectual snootiness and considered ourselves a cut above the students of other colleges.

One fine afternoon, in the Coffee House, Bishwapriya burst upon us like summer lightning. He was introduced to us by one of the members of our circle. He was of medium height, fair complexioned, well-built with a bright visage and shining eyes. He bubbled with energy and enthusiasm. He had a booming voice and a captivating smile. He made his presence immediately felt and soon became a part of our circle. He was then studying economics honours in a Central Calcutta College known as Islamia College. Bright and articulate, he had an inexhaustible repertoire of risqué jokes and regaled us by recounting them with evident joy and gusto.

Biswapriya, better known by his pet name Bhaiya, very soon became dear bhaiya to all of us and his original name was consigned to limbo. At that time debating was a rage in the Presidency College and Calcutta's academic circles. Good debaters were invariably lionized. Many sparkling debaters used to take part in debates in the Baker Laboratory Hall of the Presidency College. Names like Sudhanghsu Dasgupta, Professor Amlan Dutta, Vishwanathan and a host of others come to mind. Some of our contemporaries like Amartya Sen, Parthasarathi Gupta, Arjun Sengupta, Kamal Dutta were also renowned debaters, commanding awe and respect. Soon Bhaiya, too, blossomed as a good debater. We used to throng, whenever he was in the ring. He was witty, alert and articulate with a flair for quick repartees. Debates used to turn acrimonious on occasions and in such situations Bhaiya was at his best and finest. He often used to startle the audience with unorthodox comments and odd noises.

In our stag parties and get-togethers, Bhaiya was the cynosure of all eyes. He would steal the limelight with songs and unorthodox forms of dances. With warm young blood coursing through our veins, we would enjoy his gyrations accompanied by stupefying hoops. There were demands for encore performance and he invariably complied without much ado.

After graduation, he joined Calcutta Port Trust as an executive officer while I ploughed the old furrow and continued my studies in Calcutta University. However, he frequently visited the Coffee House and recounted interesting anecdotes regarding his varied experiences and escapades in the Calcutta Port with different odd characters including his bosses.

At that time he was courting a girl of great charm and beauty. She was one of our classmates in Presidency College. A good student and a talented danseuse, she caused flutter in many hearts. We would watch with a tinge of envy, his blossoming romance with Meenakshi, ending in a happy marriage. Meenakshi with her grace, poise and restraint was a perfect foil for Bhaiya and a great chastening influence.

Later, Bhaiya successfully competed in All-India Service Examination and joined the Indian Railway Service. Meanwhile, I had joined the Indian Police Service. Our meetings and contacts became infrequent with only chance meetings in Delhi, Calcutta and other places. He retained his inexhaustible and fierce jest for life. He remained, as before, a charming and breezy personality. As a wonderful raconteur he would recount with vivid details and great gusto his numerous confrontations with senior officers and the aftermath. Loved by his subordinates and somewhat dreaded by the seniors, as an enfant terrible he invariably and unfailingly remained helpful to all he knew. Trappings of power and authority did not turn his head or coarsen his soul. He remained quintessentially a dear old friend, whom we used to know and love since our college days.

After retirement, he settled down in Calcutta and I remained stuck in Delhi. It was Bhaiya's turn to keep the embers of our old camaraderie alive. Indifferent health and various ailments made him somewhat immobile and bed-ridden but he was invincible in spirit and soared above physical disabilities. To my joy, whenever any article of mine appeared in the columns of the Statesman he would invariably ring me up, compliment me and offer his insightful comments. To me, it was an abiding source of joy and inspiration.

Physical ailments did not dampen his spirit or blunted his mental faculties. Whenever I visited him at Calcutta with some old pals at his house in Golf Link, he would be the same warm, effusive and cordial self and never complained of physical sufferings. He remained unconquered till the end.

Last year, when Suniti rang me up and broke the news that Bhaiya has left us forever, I experienced a terrible wrench in my heart. We had lost a dear old friend forever, and will not hear anymore his booming voice, earthy jokes and searing comments on men and events. We will miss the warmth and charm he always exuded. I salute his deathless memory.

17
Our Beloved Suniti

The name of Suniti conjures up many never-to-be-forgotten memories of the past. We came from the same school. We were both students of Mitra Institution, a well-known school of Calcutta of yore days. Suniti was one year senior to me and well known in the school as a good student and an excellent sportsman. I became one of his instant admirers and looked on him as a guiding star. Our acquaintanceship gradually flowered into friendship which continued unbroken till he left us forever.

Tall, well-built with sharp and clear features and a booming voice, Suniti bestrode like a colossus. He had a natural flair for acting and superbly played the role of the hero in a drama titled "Sirajer Sapna" staged by the school students. He held us spellbound with his splendid and flawless portrayal of the leading character, young and dissolute Nawab Sirajudullah and drew loud applause from all present in the hall. He was instantly lionized, both by the teachers as well as students.

Suniti passed Matriculation examination (school Final system had not yet been introduced) with flying colours and joined Presidency College. I followed suit next year. Our meetings in college and "addas" in adjacent coffee house became much more frequent and closer bonds of camaraderie were forged. He joined the National Cadet Corps (NCC) and made his mark there with his commanding figure, proficiency in drill and parade and indomitable energy and spirit of adventure. When he used to stride in the college with his tall and smart figure draped in uniform like a knight—errant, he used to command the attention of everyone and there were flutters in the hearts of many of his female admirers. Quite a few of them fell for him.

Suniti became the General Secretary of the college union and was actively and intensely involved in different programmes and events held by the union His was a commanding presence and his supporters and admirers were many, but there were also a handful of snooty prudes, who felt that his vivacity bordering on boisterousness was not in keeping with the hoary traditions of the college.

Early fifties were our halcyon days. Calcutta was still then a beautiful city and the atmosphere in Presidency College was indeed magical. It was a bliss to be alive in that dawn. Our contemporaries in the college were some dazzling stalwarts like Amartya Sen, Sukhomay Chakravarty, Barun De and a host of others, who afterwards won national renown and international recognition. But some of the scholarly students were dry and drab individuals living in their cloistered world. Suniti was also a bright student, but he was better known for his zest for life and capacity to win friends and retain their affection.

After graduation, Suniti joined Calcutta Port Trust as a covenanted officer. I ploughed the old furrow and joined for post graduate studies in Calcutta University. Our contact, though infrequent, however, remained unbroken. After Suniti got married, we used to visit the newlyweds in their flat in north Calcutta and spend hilarious hours in their charming company. Madhusree was bright and elegant company. But malevolent destiny denied him enjoying marital bliss for long. She fell sick with an incurable ailment and remained confined to bed for years. During the entire period of her illness, Suniti remained constantly by her side and nursed her and looked after her with unflagging care and love. His patience and constancy were exemplary and showed another side of his multifaceted personality. Beneath his apparent effervescence, there was rock-like patience and steadiness.

I lost touch with him after I joined the Indian Police Service and left Calcutta. But the lost contact was renewed when I was posted in Calcutta almost after two decades as the Inspector General of the Border Security Force. Suniti was then holding a responsible and senior position in Calcutta Port Trust He later on became the Managing Director of Central Inland Waterways. He had made a name for himself as an upright officer of great professional competence and held in high esteem by all. He married again a girl of great charm and refinement. Munia was an ideal consort, who brought peace, light and joy in Suniti's life and resurrected him. Gouri and I, now and again paid visits to Suniti's quarters in Portland Park and spent many delightful evenings sipping whisky and talking about cabbages and kings. Munia was a charming hostess and endeared herself to all of us by her unfailing charm and gracious hospitality. She also made Suniti more relaxed, benign and rounded.

After my Calcutta innings I was transferred to Hyderabad and then Delhi. Contact with Suniti, however, continued uninterrupted. On retirement from service Suniti and Munia shifted to their new home in Hindustan Road. His lair now became the constant rendezvous of his old and endless friends — school and college friends, service colleagues, old childhood pals of the locality. He treated everybody with same warmth and courtesy and everybody felt the glow of his magnetism. Whenever in Calcutta it was "de rigueur' for me to visit his house on

Saturday evening and meet old friends, get lost in endless tittle-tattle and reminisce old college days. The atmosphere was pleasant and convivial. Suniti was invariably gracious and welcoming but it was Munia's warmth and hospitality which used to enliven those evenings and made us feel really at home. It was in Suniti's house I rediscovered many of my old college chums after nearly four or five decades.

Suniti's friends were legion and they came from all walks of life and had unbounded affection for him. With his love and concern for all, he attracted them like a magnet He was not just a fair-weather friend, good only for gossiping and palavering, but a true and dependable comrade in crisis and adversity. Whenever a friend encountered any serious problem or fell sick, Suniti was the first to rush to cheer him up and extend a helping hand He was indeed a 'good Samaritan'. Occasionally, I used to ring him up from Delhi and he would update me with the information about all old friends. Many, with the advance of age were keeping indifferent health and had become totally house-bound. Suniti was their constant and trusted friend in weal and woe. He would persuade them to visit his house for vitalizing "adda sessions". With jokes, hilarious anecdotes, and songs, they would be able to bury their problems and enjoy the pervasive gaiety and bonhomie.

His sudden death has left an aching void. It was like the most unexpected collapse of a towering beacon No longer it will diffuse light and joy to us all. I find it difficult even now to accept the fact that dear Suniti has left us forever and I shall no longer hear his booming voice, witty comments and feel the glow of his radiant all-conquering personality. He will always be present before our gaze like a flaming star. I shall cherish forever the ever-lasting memory of his luminous soul. My dear friend, adieu.

18
My Dear Friend Chinmoy

I first met my friend Chinmay in the National Academy of Administration, Mussorie. It was a chance meeting. Officers selected for All India Services and other Central Services are sent to the National Academy of Administration, Mussorie, for a Foundation Course lasting for five months. The basic objective behind the Course is to build up better understanding and camaraderie among officers belonging to different services, and particularly, the two All India Services — the Indian Administrative Service and Indian Police Service. It was indeed a real fun to meet and interact with officers hailing from different parts of the country with different views and outlook. Bonds of close friendship forged with some of them continue unbroken even now.

One afternoon, after lunch, when some of us were chattering in the lounge, one of our batch mates came and announced that a new IPS officer from West Bengal has just come to join the course. Out of sheer curiosity I pottered ahead to meet him. I saw a young man of fair complexion, medium height and build, cherubic face and with a beaming smile, smoking cigarette with relish and talking to another friend in Bengali in a slow and measured voice. He was explaining the reasons for his delay in joining the Foundation Course. He was serving in the West Bengal Civil Service and holding an important charge. The usual administrative lag in issuing the release order delayed his joining.

The new member of our fraternity was warmly welcomed and soon with his simple manners and easy charm Chinmoy Chakraborty became a good friend of many of us. I could in the course of time gather from him that he hailed from Barisal in East Pakistan now Bangladesh, and like many others migrated to India with his mother and sister after post-partition communal frenzy swept across the land. He lost his father at an early age and had to go through many vicissitudes of life. It was a hard grind but he kept his chin up and accepted the smiles and buffets of fortune with equal thanks. He did not become flinty or cynical. He graduated with History Honours from the Hooghly College in West Bengal and joined the West Bengal Civil Service in which he served for a couple of years before successfully competing for the Indian Police Service.

Chinmoy was simple and unassuming and was liked by all because of his candour and innate goodness. But he was, unlike many of us, very organized and methodical and blessed with a prodigious memory. He could vividly and unerringly recount the sequence and details of events of bygone days and would often correct me regarding many dates and events of history. Many of us were often overwhelmed by his command over facts.

On completion of the Foundation Course, we went to the Central Police College, Mount Abu for police training. CPTC was the acronym for constant physical torture college and, indeed, it was so. There was overwhelming emphasis on drill, parade and the probationers not proficient in drill and physical exercises were constantly derided by the trainers. They were considered as square pegs in round holes, sissies unfit for the rough and tumble of police service. A few of us, including Chinmoy, belonged to this group and were butts of snide comments and dark prophecies about our darker future in Indian Police Service. After a few months, orders of our cadre allotment came from the Home Ministry. I was allotted to Odisha cadre and Chinmoy and Kalyan Mitra, another friend, to Gujarat cadre. But later on, because of the demand of the Orissa government for more IPS officers, their cadres were changed from Gujarat to Odisha. Allotments in the same cadre forged stronger bonds between us which continue unbroken and unruffled even today.

In Odisha, after reporting at State Police Headquarters, we were sent for two months training at the Police Training College at Angul. Facilities at the PTC Angul were minimal. There were few old thatched rooms used as class rooms. The quality of the instructors was also mediocre but they were well-meaning people and used to treat us with utmost courtesy. We learned from them about the uppish behaviour of some of the young ASPs, who had earlier come for training and recalled the truth of Napoleon's saying that men forget injuries but not insults. We used to stay in a nearby building called Mission Bungalow and had a common mess. Chinmoy was in charge of the mess and ran it very competently and economically without any assistance from us, but we used to tease him by criticizing poor management, inviting from him loud and angry protests.

Though Bhuwaneshwar was the State capital, Cuttack remained the State Police Headquarters because of the reluctance of the senior police officers to leave Cuttack and move to Bhuwaneshwar. I was posted as the Assistant Superintendent of Police in Cuttack and was allotted a big bungalow. My house became a rendezvous of my batch mates whenever they visited Cuttack. I recollect many delightful evenings we spent sipping rum (whisky was beyond our means) and criticizing everything under the sun and cracking occasional risqué jokes. Chinmoy as the Assistant Superintendent of Police, Puri, and then as the Superintendent of Police, Koraput, made a name for himself and earned plaudits as a capable no-nonsense officer of unblemished integrity. He was always thorough going but at the same time a little long-winded and didactic. Once he started expatiating on a subject, it was difficult to rein in him.

As the Superintendent of Police Vigilance, Sambalpur, Chinmoy won laurels by detecting cases of huge evasion of sales tax by some unscrupulous traders and also by unearthing some sensational cases of corruption of senior public servants. I was also by that time posted as the Superintendent of Police, Vigilance, Berhampur. Our paths often crossed. We used to meet in crime meetings, police conferences and other State police functions.

From Berhampur, I went to Delhi on deputation to the Intelligence Bureau and Chinmoy also joined the Home Ministry as the Director. Many IPS officers used to approach him seeking help and favours. Many were not always happy with his even-handedness and reluctance to bend rules and regulations to bail out friends and colleagues. He was criticized unfairly by some of them for being too officious. But the criticisms were unwarranted because really he tried to help people within the framework of prescribed rules and not by stepping beyond them. He was never wooden or negative. Chinmoy ended his official career as the head of the Narcotics Control Bureau and later functioned in a UN body as a member.

Chinmoy remains a prototype of a conscientious hard working officer, who keeps our administrative machinery ticking even now. He came to India after partition as a displaced person, battled against titanic odds and reached the top of the professional ladder. Adversity steeled his character. High office did not turn his head and he remained simple, unassuming and scrupulously honest. I have seen many officers of competence and brilliance but lacking character and integrity. I admire Chinmoy's integrity and strong character and wish there are more bureaucrats like him, who are not flashy but solid, and ramrod straight. The older I grow, I judge a man more by his character than by his ideas. Chinmoy remains a shining example of a senior officer of high integrity wedded to work, inspiring others with his example of simple living and high thinking.

19
Courage and Compassion

August 16, 1946, will forever be etched in my memory. I was then a school going child. The Second World War has just ended. Great Britain, though a victor, had suffered grievous blows and was badly bruised. It was no longer in a position to lord over the colonies. The sun was setting on the British Empire.

Taik of Independence was in the air. Meetings were held and processions taken out by different political parties in Calcutta demanding immediate lowering of the Union Jack and end of the colonial rule. However, there were dark clouds on the horizon. Hindu-Muslim riots now and again were erupting in different parts of the country. There were strident demands for Pakistan by large sections of the Muslims. In schools I could see rival rallies by Hindu/Muslim students and virulent denunciation of the Congress by the Muslim League and *vice versa*. Cry for Hindu-Muslim unity of Mahatma Gandhi was falling on deaf ears. The cleavage between the two communities was widening and becoming unbridgeable.

In undivided Bengal, there was Muslim League Ministry headed by H.S. Shurawardy, a bright and charismatic Muslim leader, but wily and unscrupulous. Muslim League had declared 16th August, 1946 as a Direct Action Day for achieving the goal of Pakistan. On 27th July, 1946, the Muslim League passed a resolution revoking its earlier decision to support the Cabinet Mission Plan and opted for direct action. League leader Jinnah said, "Today we have forged a pistol and are in a position to use it". Bengal was the only Muslim majority province under the League's control. Calcutta, its Capital, was a major city from where Jinnah could prove his point.

We never thought in our wildest dreams that the Direct Action Day would turn out to be a "great killing day" and Calcutta would witness unspeakable barbarous violence and mayhem. The League Ministry had declared the day as a public holiday so that people can come out and take part in protest meetings and processions. But the Chief Minister and his henchmen had quietly and secretly worked out a Machiavellian ploy for organizing communal riots on an unprecedented scale. The Chief Minister Shurawardy visited the police control room and saw to it that the police did not intervene to stop loot and arson. The British Brigadier in charge of Law and Order in Calcutta had ordered his troops to remain confined to the barracks for the day, leaving the city naked for the rioters.

Since the morning of 16th August, many reports of attacks on Hindus in adjacent Muslim localities, gutting of Hindu shops and violent attacks on Hindu students staying in the Science College Hostel in Circular Road started pouring in. There was consternation, outrage and anger in our locality and cries for retaliatory attacks on the Muslims. Violence and fury gripped the air. Civilized behaviour and norms were beating a hasty retreat.

My father, a solicitor by profession, was a respected man in the locality. Fair, well-built and handsome, he was associated with many local clubs and commanded, awe and respect. He was also a man of immense courage. Just in front of our house, there were some *bustees* inhabited by some Muslim rickshaw pullers and coach men. Many of them used to visit our house and we used to know them by their first names. My father intuitively guessed that very soon communal fire would spread in our predominantly Hindu locality. The storm was gathering and about to break out with savage fury. He felt that the poor and innocent Muslims staying in the bustees would soon become the victims of insensate mob fury. In order to ensure their safety, they have to be dispatched to nearby Muslim localities. He summoned some of the local boys and forming a cordon under his leadership, he escorted them to a predominantly Muslim locality. Some of the youngsters were demurring but they could not say no to my father. They had to abide by his decision.

Events soon proved how right he was. By evening, entire Calcutta was in flames. Hindu mobs had also started to retaliate. Howling mobs gathered before the bustees in front of our house intending to butcher the innocent Muslims. But they could find none. They had already been spirited away. My father's noble spirit and presence of mind had saved the lives of those innocent people and redeemed the honour of the locality.

There were genuine apprehensions that at night Muslim ruffians may attack Hindu localities. My father was in the forefront of organizing the local defence and mobilizing the young men of the area to remain alert to fend off any such incursions. He was leading from the front.

On 17th August, Army was called in and peace and order limped back to the benighted city after a couple of days. The leading national daily *Statesman*, in a powerful editorial, which I still recollect, called it "Great Killing Day" and compared it to a medieval fury. It lambasted the Muslim League administration and the British Governor Sir Fredrick Burrows for abdicating their responsibilities and allowing this monstrous communal violence taking toll of many innocent lives and creating unbridgeable chasm between the two communities.

Gory riots on 16th August in Calcutta triggered communal riots all over the country, ultimately leading to its vivisection. Even now, after six decades, when I recollect that blood-soaked day, I see before my mind's eye, the picture of my father standing tall and upright, representing the voice of sanity and courage in the midst of enveloping darkness.

20
A Touching Gesture

It was a cold wintry night in Delhi in December, 1977. I was at that time posted as the Deputy Inspector General in charge of investigation in the Shah Commission of Enquiry set up by the then Janata Government to enquire into the subversion of lawful processes and established conventions and various other excesses committed during the period of emergency proclaimed by Smt. Indira Gandhi. Emergency was a calculated assault on Indian democracy and many excesses were perpetrated by the minions of the government during this period. Pent-up anger and frustration of the public burst forth with the end of emergency. Thousands of complaints poured into the Commission from all parts of the country. Selected complaints were dealt with by the Commission through its own investigative agency. The Commission also took up for open hearing some cases in which there had been blatant abuse of authority and misuse of power and the excesses committed were of gravest magnitude.

Justice Shah was a no-nonsense judge of robust integrity. Fair complexioned, tall and taciturn, Shah was an epitome of judicial propriety and conducted himself with sublime dignity. He had a clear razor-sharp and organized mind and used to dictate orders after every hearing with remarkable clarity. He wanted to finish the work of the Commission within a time frame. He was dead set against, unlike many other retired judges, seeking any extension of the time period of the Commission.

The Secretary of the Commission, P.R. Rajgopal, former Commissioner of Police, Delhi, was a well known and reputed officer, who commanded respect and wholesome awe of the subordinates. He was a martinet, who would brook no nonsense and make no compromise in spheres of work and discipline, but at the same time, he was warm and considerate. He also was a hustler driving us hard to accomplish the mission within one year time span of the commission. Both he and Justice Shah were at the same time very clear that our investigation work should be transparent and above board and must not be soiled by dubious and questionable methods. To a large extent, this could be realized. Though political controversies dogged the steps of the Commission, there had not been any criticisms against the nature and style of functioning of the investigating wing. Not even its harshest critics could point out instances of biased and motivated investigation by the officers.

In the Commission, I was in charge of the team enquiring into the excesses committed in Haryana during the Emergency. Bansilal, the Chief Minister of Haryana during emergency, was a go-getter but adopted many highhanded and unethical means to achieve his political ends. He was an acolyte of Sanjay Gandhi and went extra miles to curry favour with him. He commanded fierce loyalty as well as unmitigated hatred. The work in the Commission was both challenging as well as exhausting. Voluminous papers and complaints had to be pored over. Many witnesses had to be questioned and veracity of their submissions checked up.

One day, while when I was working in the Commission my wife Gouri rang up and said that my younger son was experiencing abdominal pain since morning and getting no relief even after taking some pain-killing tablets. Returning home in the evening, both of us took the child to the nearby Safdurjung Hospital. The glum-faced insensitive doctor, who examined the child was not able to diagnose the ailment and only said that the child has to be kept under further observation for a few more hours before diagnosing the precise nature of the ailment. With this solemn, pronouncement he vanished from the room and did not return. The child was writhing in pain. Gouri was in tears and I was at my wit's end, petrified by anxiety and not knowing what is to be done. In that moment of despair I rang up the Secretary of the Commission Rajgopal at his residence. He was not there. I left a message that on his return he may kindly ring me back at the hospital. Within an hour Rajgopal rang me back. I narrated to him my dire predicament. His response was instantaneous. He assured me and said that he himself was coming to the hospital with a doctor. And true to his word, he arrived with a specialist, who examined my son and said that it was a case of acute appendicitis, a rare and uncommon ailment for a child and suggested immediate operation.

At Rajgopal's request, the child specialist himself did the operation successfully. After operation the doctor told me that it was indeed a close shave. Any further delay would have made the operation hazardous and endangered the child's life. It was indeed a touch and go. My son had to stay in the hospital for a few more days and then returned home. Soon he was his old self.

Even now almost after four decades, whenever I think of Rajgopal, ineffaceable memories of that evening flash back to my mind. In that dark evening in the gloomy surroundings of the hospital, Rajgopal appeared like a benign saviour, not a tough office boss but a warm-hearted and compassionate leader with deep concern for the subordinate officers. This kind of spontaneous and never-to-be forgotten gesture cements unbreakable bonds between the team leader and his men. Indeed, Rajgopal was a wonderful leader and a grand coordinator. When I turned to him to express my grateful thanks, he just said, "*repeat to your subordinates when they turn to you for help in their moments of distress*".

21
Cop on the Beat

In the police hierarchy, the position of the constables is lowly and lost. Though they form the base of the pyramid, they are viewed as hewers of wood and drawers of water and often looked down upon by the senior officers. The Police Commission 1902, appointed by Lord Curzon (*the first All India Commission to view holistically police issues and problems all over the country*) recommended for them a mechanical role, where the constables would not have to exercise any judgment or discretion. Most of them were ill-trained and poorly educated and served the role of errand boys. The situation has not changed since then.

The cardinal fact is forgotten that the constabulary represents the image of the police before the public. Their amiability, courtesy and competence endear, while their misconduct and lapses sully the image of the police. The constable remains, as a perceptive author has put it, a spear carrier at the background of the police drama and not a major actor standing in the centre stage.

The ill-paid and ill-trained constabulary constitutes the Achilles heel of the Indian police. Very little has been done despite salutary recommendations by many Police Commissions and Committees to set things right. Their promotion prospects are bleak. Many constables all over the country, after 30 or 35 years of service, retire in the same rank. They see no flicker of light at the end of the tunnel and retire sullen and crestfallen. This is extremely frustrating.

But constables, if well led and duly empowered, can render yeoman service to the force. Indeed, some display remarkable presence of mind, strength of character and leadership qualities and constitute an untapped and unexplored reservoir of strength.

My mind goes back to a remarkable incident in 1979 when the country witnessed a bewildering but grim spectacle of policemen going on strike. A section of the media called it a police mutiny. The agitation began in the Punjab and then spread like prairie fire to other States. Causes were many genuine and unredressed grievances of the constables. The simmering discontent soon took a turbulent agitational form. I was at that time posted as Range DIG, Rourkela in Orissa. Initially, there was no visible turmoil among the police forces in Orissa, but this was deceptive. There were currents of smouldering discontent and tension. But the police hierarchy did not hear the rumblings of the distant thunder.

I held an *alochana sabha* with the senior officers and the constables of the Rourkela district with a view to providing some sort of a safety valve to the constabulary to unburden themselves and ventilate their grievances. The constables during discussions clamoured for payment of compensatory allowance (which they used to get at the initial stage of Rourkela Steel Plant's construction) and better housing and medical facilities. These were long-pending grievances.

The police leadership was not in a position to redress them without positive response from the State government as they had long-term financial implications. The constables, however, held the cards close to their chest and did not give any inkling of any agitational programme they were soon going to launch. In Orissa, police agitation took the form of policemen not reporting for duties in different districts, but it did not take a violent or volatile turn. The peaceful disposition of the Oriya people and the bonds of understanding between police leaders and the constabulary in many districts, prevented any ominous or violent turn of the agitation. The Orissa Police, though defiant, were not, unlike some other States, politicized or unionized.

Agitation of the Central Industrial Security Force (CISF) posted in the Rourkela Steel Plant was however spiralling out of control and snowballing into an ominous maelstrom. CISF jawans in the Bokaro Steel Plant fought gun battles with army contingents and had to be forcibly disarmed. There were fears that the Bokaro story may be repeated at Rourkela Steel Plant. Fortunately, that tragic denouement could be avoided. Thanks to timely intervention by police and plant authorities and arrival of BSF contingent from Kolkata, the charged situation could be defused without any violent confrontation. Police agitation also gradually died down all over the country. State governments adopted a carrot-and-stick policy. In Orissa, some of the ring leaders of the agitation were dismissed from service by invoking Article 311(2) of the Constitution, but they were subsequently reinstated by the State government as a gesture of clemency.

In Rourkela, during the agitation a remarkable incident occurred, which I vividly recollect even today. The sepoys of Orissa Military Police battalion stationed at Rourkela staged a protest march following the misbehaviour of the police commandant towards a sepoy. In the parade ground, the commandant, in a flash of ill-controlled temper grabbed the neck of a sepoy and admonished him. It was like a spark on a dry timber. The angry gesticulating sepoys came out in a protest march and gathered at the centre of the city. The District Superintendent of Police and the District Magistrate came to my office and informed me of these unseemly developments. Both of them felt that as the senior-most police officer I should personally talk to them. I immediately agreed. Arriving at the scene, I found that the police men were seething with anger at the ignominy suffered by a fellow sepoy. They were loudly venting their grievances and raising angry slogans. Meanwhile, a big crowd had gathered to witness the strange spectacle of a disciplined force behaving like a rabble. Some of their self-styled leaders were acting as rabble-rousers.

My initial efforts to pacify them by promising to look into their grievances and taking disciplinary action against the errant officer were not successful. The protesting constables were defiant and in no mood to listen. The efforts of SP, District Magistrate and the local MLA, who had also arrived on the scene to pacify them, made no headway. The situation was slipping out of hand. While I was thinking of an alternative strategy, a young constable of the local police station with a bright face and sparkling eyes came to my rescue and took up the cudgels on my behalf. In a clear unfaltering voice he admonished his battalion colleagues for bringing police to disrepute by creating an unseemly imbroglio. He strongly urged them to go back to the barracks without creating any more public scene and making a mockery of police discipline. The protesting constables were taken aback by the sharp reproof by one of their colleague. There was a lull. Admonition by the colleague had some cooling and sobering effect. Taking advantage of the situation, I again spoke to the agitators reiterating my promise of a full scale enquiry into the grievances and succeeded this time in persuading them to go back to their barracks. It was the end of a horrid nightmare.

I now turned to the hero of the hour, who displayed the finest qualities of a police officer and a crisis manager. He did not speak a word. Quiet and self-possessed, he listened to my congratulatory remarks and then clicked his heels, gave a smart salute and walked away with due grace and dignity.

When I think of that episode I experience in the depths of my heart a twinge of sorrow and remorse. Indeed, as police officers we have failed to empower the constabulary and help them in terms of career advancement. This is one of our marked failures to provide proper and inspiring leadership to the force. Many of us are indeed lost leaders.

22

Zero to Hero

Sometimes the best as well as the worst traits of a man's character are revealed in difficult and challenging situations. A man deemed unworthy and incompetent can display courage and presence of mind unexpected of him and similarly one considered strong and lion-hearted becomes craven in a crisis. I recall a revealing incident when an officer considered inept showed his true métier in a life-and-death situation. Details of the incident were recounted to me by a close friend and colleague.

My friend Kalyan Mitra was posted as the Superintendent of Police in Bolangir district of Orissa. It was his first district charge. As new SP, he was straining hard to get to grips with the problems of effectively policing a district and earn his spurs. One of the foremost challenges of a SP in a district is to size up his subordinates, assess their strong and weak points and then make suitable job allocations. His success as the police chief of the district depends much on the choice of his team and the way in which he leads the team.

In a district police organization, reserve office is the key-stone of the arch. It is the nerve centre for deployment of police personnel for various duties all over the district. For quick response to emergencies, the district armed police reserve is stationed in the reserve office. The Reserve Inspector is an important functionary, whose job is to ensure efficient running of the reserve office and also to organize sports, drills and games in the reserve ground. He has a pivotal role to play in smooth deployment and maintenance of discipline in the force.

Mitra's reserve inspector at that time was one Binod Mohanty. He was smart, muscular with an athletic bearing. But performance of duties belied his smart appearance. He was casual, laidback and somewhat mercurial. Duties assigned to him were perfunctorily performed and he had to be pulled up on countless occasions for various omissions and commissions. But censures and remonstrances did not have any visible impact on him. Mohanty remained unredeemed.

But in an extraordinary situation, the same Mohanty, who was often the butt of Mitra's invectives displayed exemplary courage and presence of the mind of a high order never expected of him. Lousinga Police Station of Bolangir district, at that time, was terrorized by a leopard wreaking havoc. The grisly animal had become a byword of fear. Many panic-stricken villagers had left their villages and sought the help of the district authorities to protect them from the leopard menace. Responding to the call of duty, the young Superintendent of Police went to the village, accompanied by a constable, who was an ace shooter and the reserve Inspector Mohanty. Mitra felt that as a young S.P. he must lead from the front. Reaching the village, Mitra came to know from the villagers that the leopard after being shot and wounded by a local Shikari had retreated into a nearby forest. In his fervid enthusiasm, he committed an error of judgement by deciding to enter the forest in search of the leopard accompanied by the reserve Inspector Mohanty and the constable, who was an ace rifle shooter of the district. Mohanty, was carrying a 410 musket and Mitra and the constable carried 303 rifles each. Just entering the forest, the party heard a deafening growl and saw the animal glaring at them at a distance of about 25 feet. Before Mitra could press the trigger, the animal rushed towards him in a lightning burst of speed and pounced on him. The rifle flew away from his hands and he fell on the ground with his face turning upwards. The constable thinking that discretion was the better part of valour took to his heels, hid himself under a tree and watched the proceedings from a distance. But Mohanty held his nerve and came to Mitra's rescue. He repeatedly tried to hit the animal with the barrel of the gun and went on shouting to distract its attention. The angry leopard, which was trying to claw prostrate Mitra by one hand and snarl at Mohanty, suddenly gave up the prey and moved to a nearby bush. Mohanty lifted the SP, who had suffered injuries in several parts of the body and was profusely bleeding. Providentially, he was safe and alive.

Later, Mohanty was awarded the "*Prime Minister's Medal for life saving*". The Orissa Government's letter recommending the award said that "*Had the Inspector displayed the normal instinct of self-preservation and not rushed with an empty musket to physically obstruct and ward off the injured animal in a desperate effort to save the life of SP, things would have been different.*"

Later, when Mitra asked him why he risked his own life, to save the life of S.P., he said "*Sir, how could I leave you lying on the ground with the animal charging at you, I had to remain by your side, come what may*". The young Inspector, who was often pulled up and sermonized for omissions and misjudgements displayed at a crucial moment extraordinary courage, and loyalty of the highest order. He towered above many, who belittled him and showed that how fallible can be our assessment and judgment of men, who work by our side day in and day out. There are occasions, as the biblical saying goes, when the stone which the builder rejects becomes the head of the church.

23
Owning Up Omissions

The responsibility of the Border Security Force (BSF) to guard the country's borders is a daunting one. After India-Pakistan war of 1965, the Government of India decided that guarding of the far-flung, ill-demarcated and porous border of the country should be done not by the regular army but by Para-military forces so that armies of the two neighbouring countries do not snarl at each other across the border and create combustible situations. In the eastern front, the long porous border of 2230 km with Bangladesh starting from sub-Himalayan terrain of Cooch Bihar in the North and extending to the south upto the mouth of Bay of Bengal posed different but difficult problems. The boundary line does not follow any natural geographical alignment. It moves in a criss-cross manner through the densely populated villages, long green paddy fields and innumerable seasonal and perennial rivers and nullas. At the time of country's partition, the boundary line drawn by Rad Cliffe Commission was hastily implemented on the ground due to paucity of time without proper field visit or examination. The result was chaotic. Indeed, it was made historically possible what is geographically impossible. A number of villages extend upto the zero line of the border, and strangely enough, there are bordering villages with parts of them in India, and parts in Bangladesh.

Though the border with Bangladesh remains by and large soft and peaceful, the task of BSF officers and men guarding the border does not become less daunting. In most of the bordering areas of West Bengal, there are no lateral roads running across the border. During the monsoon and post-monsoon period, many of these areas become waterlogged and inaccessible and patrolling the border becomes a difficult as well as irksome job. Open and porous border encourages smuggling and infiltration. In smuggling, BSF personnel as well as their counterparts of Bangladesh Rifles (BDR), the Para-military force guarding Bangladesh border, get trapped. Some of them, including their officers, develop unholy nexus with these smugglers. Smuggling is indeed a thriving and lucrative business. Many villagers on both sides of the border earn their livelihood through smuggling. At times, clashes would take place between BSF men and villagers involved in smuggling. Most of the BSF officers and men, who patrol the border are from North Indian States and do not know the local language and mores. They are, at times, heavy handed and trigger-happy and contemptuous of impoverished local villagers.

I still recollect with horror a gory incident that had occurred in the village of Debnathpur in Nadia district on 19th March 1991. I was then posted as Inspector General of BSF in Kolkata. Following an altercation with a BSF patrolling party a group of villagers aided and abetted by smugglers surrounded them and confined them in a room. Hearing the news a rescue party was rushed from battalion headquarters. After rescuing the confined BSF personnel, the enraged BSF jawans wanted to teach a bitter lesson to the captors and opened fire on the villagers in which 11 were killed and 2 injured. It was unprovoked, uncontrolled and indiscriminate firing with a view to striking terror in the minds of the recalcitrant villagers. Hearing the news, I rushed post-haste from my Headquarters in Kolkatta. When I arrived at the spot, I could see that the enraged BSF jawans had chased the villagers and opened fire on them inside the shops and houses. Blood was spattered everywhere. The assembled villagers led by some political leaders were hopping mad and demanding immediate criminal action against the delinquent BSF Jawans and reparations to the victims' family members.

I sat down with the villagers along with A.S. Beddi, DIG, BSF, who accompanied me and patiently heard from the villagers a blow-by-blow account of the gory incident. I told the villagers that it was erroneous on their part to confine the BSF jawans, but it was totally unjustified on the part of the BSF personnel, despite the provocation, to forget their training, discipline and cause this blood bath by resorting to this disproportionate use of force.

I promised to prosecute them under relevant provisions of BSF act and impose on the delinquent staff deterrent punishment. I assured them of some financial assistance to the victim's families from the BSF welfare fund. I also promised to provide jobs to the family members of the deceased villagers in the BSF. This had a calming effect and the tension-charged situation could be defused. While I was parleying with the villagers, the Home Secretary, Government of West Bengal rang up to communicate that the Chief Minister Jyoti Basu desired that the delinquent BSF staff should be handed over to the police for criminal prosecution for committing manslaughter. I disagreed and said that the aberrant staff will be dealt with under the BSF Act which contains stringent provisions of punishment instead of handing them over to the police, to suffer long drawn trial in the court of law. Our action will be swift as well as deterrent. Local CPM leaders, including a Minister, did not like my stand and accused me of shielding the BSF staff.

I called a press conference in Kolkata on my return. It was a crowded conference. Representatives of all the leading newspapers of Kolkata, as well as the electronic media were present. I had to face a volley of searching questions. I candidly admitted that BSF firing was unjustified and unprovoked and trigger happy jawans and their supervisors will be dealt with under the BSF Act and visited with deterrent punishment. I conceded that there were, as in any other organization, some bad apples in the BSF, who have had links with the smugglers and criminals and we are launching steps to weed them out. Discussions in the press conference were widely covered in both print and electronic media. There were criticism of BSF operations in the border areas and their collusion with the smugglers. But my stand of owning up our lapses in public instead of defending the indefensible conduct of our staff was appreciated. The members of the public also endorsed my stand and appreciated the gesture to help the victims' families.

There were criticisms from within the organization that I have owned up before the public, misconduct and misuse of the force by the BSF even before holding an enquiry under the BSF Act. I should have suspended my judgement and taken a decision only after conclusion of an enquiry. But I felt that it was better to face the truth and eventual outcome instead of taking recourse to a purblind official stance. Truth has its own strength and it is better to openly admit the lapses and make amends.

Fortunately, the then Director General of BSF, H.P. Bhatnagar backed my stand and advised me to organize training programmes of the BSF personnel and meetings with the border population so that there is better rapport between BSF and the villagers. This was done in a regular and systematic manner and incidents of clashes between the villagers and the BSF men came down.

After a week, I called on Jyoti Basu, the Chief Minister of West Bengal at the Writers Building. The Chief Secretary, Krishnamurty told me that he was quite angry and upset. However, I found him in a mellowed mood. He, as usual was very courteous and did not display any irritation. He wanted to know the action taken against the defaulting BSF staff so that he could explain the situation to the people of the areas, who were coming to meet him. He appreciated the measures taken by me and said that there should be no repetition of similar incidents.

24

VIP Security

A Thankless Job

One of the difficult and irksome jobs of the police is performance of VIP security duties. It is thankless and can be at times very frustrating. During the last four decades in India, VIP security problems have increased exponentially and made the task of those in charge of VIP protection very daunting. Terrorism stalks the land. Two of our Prime Ministers had fallen victims to terrorist attacks and many other important public figures remain constantly exposed to serious security threats and require constant protection. Some of the VIPs are paranoid and some look upon the security protection as a status symbol and try to flaunt it brazenly, forgetting the revulsion it causes in public mind. Again, there are some, who suffer from an advanced sense of megalomania and instead of cooperating and helping the security staff deployed for their protection, create various odd problems, and in the process, expose themselves and the staff to avoidable security threats. Trapped in power and authority, they tend to feel that they are darlings of the crowd, who gather or are collected to hear them and the police and the security staff only create barriers between them and the crowd.

It is also true that sometimes VIP security staff display

insensitivity and poor professionalism, but the VIPs tend to forget that those in charge of their protection will feel confused and demoralized if they are not treated with due civility and directed to depart from laid down rules and procedures, compounding in the process, risks to the VIPs. I, too had to face such piquant situations in my police career. One incident remains vivid in my mind. I was then posted as the Deputy Inspector General of Police of the Western Range, in Rourkela, Orissa. The then President of India, Sanjeeva Reddy visited Rourkela to attend a function of the Rourkela Steel Plant.

It was an interesting and exciting time. The Janata government at the centre had suffered a humiliating defeat in the election and the Congress led by Smt. Indira Gandhi stormed back to power. The present President of the country Pranab Mukherjee, the Minister in Charge of Commerce, came with Sanjeeva Reddy as the Minister-in-waiting. He impressed us all with his pleasant manners, clarity of thinking and command over facts and figures.

The President stayed in the Rourkela House, the main guest house of the Steel Plant. There was a congregation of VIPs, including, the Chief Minister of Orissa J.B. Patnaik and other leading lights of his ministry. Senior officers of the Steel Authority of India, important bureaucrats of the Central and State government, and hordes of lesser luminaries had assembled on the occasion. It was a real jamboree and a lot of confusion prevailed all-around. The Managing Director of the Steel Plant, Dr. Datar, a competent professional, was a harassed and beleaguered man. I remember I quoted to him the well known lines of the Gondoliers:

> "In short, whoever you may be,
> to this conclusion you may agree,

when anyone is somebody,
there is no one's anybody".

He had a hearty laugh.

The Government of India has laid down detailed security instructions regarding procedures to be observed during the visits of the President and the Prime Minister. These have been encapsulated in a booklet known as the Blue Book. These instructions have to be adhered strictly and any carelessness and negligence in their observance by the police and the security personnel was seriously frowned upon and senior officers were held personally responsible. But the security problems are often compounded by mock heroic and thoughtless actions of the VIPs, who chafe at the security restrictions and feel that the police were needlessly creating a gulf between them and the crowd.

As per the instruction of the Blue Book, an elaborate security drill after the President's arrival at the Rourkela air strip had been worked out and thoroughly rehearsed. At the Rourkela air strip, a small crowd had gathered to welcome the President. Some of the cheerleaders welcomed the President, shouted slogans and waved banners when he alighted from the aircraft. President Sanjeeva Reddy felt happy and thrilled by crowd's response and all of a sudden asked the driver of the vehicle to change the car route and take him nearer to the sections of the crowd waving flags and loudly chanting welcoming slogans. The driver of the vehicle was flummoxed and did not know what to do. I was travelling in the same vehicle with the President and respectfully pointed out to him that the car route may not be changed all of a sudden. Taking exception at my intervention, he brusquely told me not to stand between him and the public. He lost sight of the fact that the drills and the precautions were not arbitrary and had been meticulously worked out to safeguard the security of the

VIPs. In view of his insistence, I had no other option but to remain silent. Fortunately, the visit passed off peacefully, but in a report to the State Police Headquarters, I pointed out the security problems that could be posed by the VIPs. I cited an interesting case study which showed how impromptu changes of routes could be hazardous for the VIPs. In this connection, I mentioned that the murder of Arch Duke of Austria at Sarajevo on June 28, 1914 (the fatal spark that ignited the First World War) was possible because the military governor of Bosnia had directed the return journey by another route. The Arch Duke's car halted in a wrong place and this gave an opportunity to the assassins, who were following him, to open fire on him and his consort, killing them both. However, one does not know how and when the mindset of our VIPs is going to change. VIP protection must seek to avoid unnecessary and uncalled for restrictions on the people. But the VIPs also by their stubbornness and petulance must not compromise their own security and make the work of the police more difficult.

25
Mistaken Identity

I was posted as the Deputy Inspector General in the Shah Commission of Enquiry set up to enquire into the excesses perpetrated during the Emergency. I was given the responsibility of investigating some serious cases of gross abuse of police authority and harassment of people owing allegiance to opposition parties. The dreary and painstaking investigation work in Haryana was not without comic interludes. Once while camping at the headquarters of Hissar district, I wanted to visit the new Agricultural University at Hissar and informed the district authorities accordingly. My limited intention was to get a bird's eye view of the sprawling university complex. However, by a strange quirk of fate, I was overwhelmed by some unexpected and unanticipated events. To my surprise, I found that the Vice-Chancellor of the University was waiting for me in the portico of the administrative building. Before I could open my mouth, he started 'sirring' me profusely and said that he would take me round the university complex. For the next two hours, the situation turned out to be really Gilbertian. The Vice-Chancellor explained to me with great enthusiasm the various achievements of the University. An obliging cameraman appeared from nowhere and started clicking the camera. Accompanied by the Vice-Chancellor, I visited the different faculties of the University and the heads of the departments vied with one another in explaining to me in all earnestness the latest researches that were being carried out in different departments of the University. I made some amiable, though perhaps not exactly appropriate, remarks. While I was taken round the spacious, redbrick library building, the librarian asked me to record my name and enter my remarks in the visitors' register. After I had written my name in the visitors' register, I could notice a distinct change in the Vice-Chancellor's manner. He became a little stiff and stand-offish, and after a little while abruptly took leave of me. I could sense that something had gone seriously wrong somewhere. The red-carpet welcome and its abrupt end remained to me a riddle wrapped in mystery. I got the answer when later on, my friend, who was then the Range DIG, Hissar told me that someone not kindly disposed towards the Vice-Chancellor, with a puckish sense of humour, had sent a message to him that Justice Shah, Chairman of the Commission, would be visiting the university. It was a classic case of mistaken identity.

26
Femme Fatale

During my long years in police profession, I had occasions to investigate and supervise many difficult and sensational crimes showing human depravity at the lowest. Greed, lust, vengeance, wounded vanity, psychological maladjustments are some of the important causative factors behind commission of these gruesome crimes. But there are instances where a weak and feckless man, under the malevolent influence of a strong-willed vengeful woman is prompted to commit crimes against his better judgement. There are Lady Machbeths in real life.

I have had the occasion to supervise such a case when I was the Deputy Inspector General in the Criminal Investigation Department of Odisha Police. The hideous event took place at NALCO Nagar (a township of National Aluminium Corporation of India) in Dhenkanal district of Odisha. A report was received by the local police of the brutal murder of the wife of an Assistant Engineer of the NALCO and her two little children. There were several stab injuries on the body of the young lady and the throats of two little children were slit by a sharp-cutting weapon. Due to the sensational nature of the crime and the public outcry that followed, the investigation of the case had to be taken up by the Crime Branch of the Odisha Police. Normally, in State police organizations knotty and sensational cases are handed over to the State CID.

During investigation of the case, the CID officers found that the peon Padmacharan Behera and his wife Parvati staying in the outhouse of the quarters of the Assistant Engineer S. Subramaniam were missing. Padmacharan was functioning as an office peon and an errand boy while Parvati as a maid servant cooked food and performed other domestic chores. When I met and interviewed Subramaniam, I found that he was stupefied by the grim tragedy and was totally numbed and dazed. Silent and disobedient tears rolled down his cheeks. Suspicion naturally fell on the fugitive Padmacharan and his wife Parvati for commission of the murder and theft of golden ornaments and other articles from the house.

Search for the fugitives began in right earnest. Inspectors of the Crime Branch first rushed to the native place of Padmacharan at Tileshwar in Phulbani district of Odisha and could learn that Padmacharan and Parvati had not come there. They discovered that Padmacharan had a first wife. Padmacharan's first wife and parents said that they were completely in the dark about Padmacharan's whereabouts. The determined and indefatigable officers of the Crime Branch without any further loss of time dashed for Parvati's native place in Midnapore district in West Bengal. There they were able to apprehend Padmacharan and Parvati. The couple were completely taken aback as they could never imagine that the Crime Branch officers would dog the trail and apprehend them in their lair at Midnapore. During interrogation Padmacharan made a clean-breast confession of the crime. He said that while serving in Subramaniam's house as peon he came to know Parvati, the Bengali maid working there. Parvati was good-looking and physically attractive. Padmacharan soon came completely under the bewitching spell of Parvati and turned to a puppet under her total control. Parvati was strong-willed and temperamental. Parvati was not getting along well with Subramaniam's wife Jenova, who used to often scold her for shoddy and perfunctory working. Padmacharan also was getting annoyed with Subramaniam and doubted that the latter was casting covetous glances on Parvati. Parvati also resented Jenova's remonstrances and nursed deep anger against her. This smouldering anger, which consumed her, soon took the form of a desire for revenge. She wanted to do away with Jenova. The femme fatale started goading besotted Padmacharan to murder Jenova and run away with all her valuables. Padmacharan initially tried to disabuse her mind of such gory and fiendish ideas, but Parvati was strong-willed and a temptress. Padmacharan, who had become a puppet in her hand, gave in. Like Lady Macbeth, she prevailed over Padmacharan to execute her diabolical plans.

When Subramaniam went alone to attend a family function at Tamil Nadu, Parvati and Padmacharan felt that this was the propitious time to carry out their macabre scheme. On the night of 24th July 1984, Parvati slept in the house along with Jenova and the two children. As per prearranged plan, Parvati at the dead of night opened the door from inside. Padmacharan tiptoed in with a long sharp knife which he had borrowed from a neighbour for slicing vegetables. Padmacharan and Parvati first strangled Jenova to death and slit the throats of two children when cries of alarm broke out from them. Parvati's lust for lucre was overwhelming and insatiable. She removed the golden nose flowers and ear rings from the dead body of Jenova. They then ransacked the bedroom and decamped with other valuables.

During her interrogation before the police, Parvati candidly stated that she had decided to start a new life with Padmacharan because he showed love and sympathy for her, when she was ill-treated by her first husband. She, however, stated that

Padmacharan never divulged to her that he was already married. She admitted that rebukes and insults heaped on her daily by Jenova had become unbearable. She could not suffer the ignominy any longer and wanted to settle score with Jenova by killing her. They did not intend to kill the innocent children but had no other alternative when they raised an alarm. Both said that by no stretch of the imagination they could think that police officers from Odisha would dog their trail and catch them at Midnapore. After thorough investigation, the crime branch officers gathered every bit of evidence and submitted charge-sheet. In the test identification parade, Subramaniam identified the stolen articles. The blood stains on the seized knife contained blood group B which matched with that of Jenova and one of the two murdered sons. During the trial the defense took the plea that Subramaniam was present in the house on the fateful night and it was he, who murdered Jenova and his two sons because of his lust for Parvati. This untenable plea was rejected by the court and the Sessions Judge convicted Padmacharan and Parvati under Section 302 IPC and sentenced them to rigorous imprisonment for life.

A vengeful and passionate woman's smouldering rage and lust for gold and lucre was responsible for this dastardly crime. Three innocent lives were snuffed out. Life of a young engineer was shattered. I do not know if he was later on able to overcome the shattering blow and move on. "*The hell knoweth no fury*", as the bard of Avon has said, "*than a woman scorned*". A strong-willed woman made a weak man a plaything in the commission of a terrible crime.

27
Perennially Young

There are some people who remain ever-young and ever-inspiring. Age does not wither or stale their physical and mental faculties. On the other hand, with advance in age they become more gracious, positive and proactive. B.S. Das, one of the senior-most members of the Indian Police Service, is a wonderful and inspiring specimen of this rare breed. I first met him in a meeting of the Association of Senior Retired Indian Police Service Officers (ASRIPSO) in Delhi. He was one of the guiding spirits behind the formation of the Association for promoting professional deliberations among the retired police and security professionals and facilitating social intercourse among the families of the same fraternity.

Das has had a chequered and successful service career. He joined the Indian Police Service in its first batch in 1948 and was allotted the UP cadre. He held a few important and challenging charges. He was a successful Superintendent of Police of some trouble-prone districts. He commanded the loyalty of the subordinates and won affection of the members of the public by his amiable and civilized behaviour and leadership qualities. His seniors liked him for his professionalism and commitment and juniors admired him for his charismatic leadership. But the rough and tumble of the police job was not his métier. He yearned for a different life and wanted to step out of the narrow confines of the districts and see the glory and splendour of the world.

He went on secondment to the Indian Foreign Service and commenced an altogether new but very successful innings. He served in London, Moscow and later on as Indian Ambassador in Bhutan. He also held subsequently the challenging job of the Managing Director of Air India.

In his recently published autobiographical narrative *Memoirs of an Indian Diplomat*, Das narrates his roller-coaster ride and mentions how he had to carry the cross because of his police background. He was viewed sometimes as a *persona non-grata* and some of the stalwarts of Indian Foreign Service initially cold shouldered him and later on came to appreciate the sterling qualities of his mind and character and reposed full trust in him. He was posted as the Indian Special Officer in Bhutan and Chief Administrator, Sikkim, and displayed diplomatic skill of a high order.

He also had a stormy innings as the Managing Director, Air India during the emergency and was unceremoniously bundled out by Sanjay Gandhi and his cronies. In an interesting chapter in his book *Air India in Disarray*, he has vividly described about how corruption, mismanagement and constant political and bureaucratic interference eroded the autonomy of Air India and hastened its decline. Even now, according to him, Air India has some best technical and non-technical staff but it lacks leadership.

Das has played a key role in strengthening and galvanizing ARSIPSO. When the President of ARSIPSO, A.K. Dave, another stalwart of Indian Police, suddenly expired, Das stepped into his shoes as the President. I was a member of the Executive Committee and got the opportunity to know and frequently interact with him. Das in his early eighties was the senior most member of our group but was most proactive and dynamic in his thoughts and outlook. He sincerely felt that retired officers of Indian Police Service who, in their respective service careers held high offices with distinction in different capacities constitute a pool of unmatched expertise in spheres of law enforcement, national security and intelligence. It will be a crowning pity if they hang up their boots, and become whiners, living in the world of yesterdays and fail to put in some use their knowledge and expertise. At a time when the country faces security threats of gravest magnitudes they cannot afford to be lotus eaters. They should constitute a think tank and step forward to help the government and the society with well-thought-out and practical ideas and insights. He often quotes the example of Indian Diplomats Association where the retired groups of Indian Foreign Service officers study and examine in depth various issues relating to external affairs and provide useful inputs to the government. But in ARSIPSO, there are many Jeremiahs who feel that our innings is over and the Association should confine itself to pleasant, social get-togethers and functions and not concern itself with issues of governance. There are others to do the job. The debate rages and the Association is impaled on the horns of a dilemma.

Das has always remained a gentleman to his fingertips and generous to a fault. He is unfailingly gracious and has a knack of putting people at ease with his disarming candour. These shining qualities of head and heart endeared him to all with whom he worked and earned plaudits from many quarters.

Now in his mid-eighties, he remains a picture of grace and poise and exudes a benign charm. His accomplished wife Smt. Nirmala Das was a source of great strength and inspiration to him and her death was a grievous loss. The personal tragedy saddened and subdued him but did not douse his jest for life. He remains as before positive, alert and full of beans. He constantly exhorts ARSIPSO members to make it a more vibrant and dynamic organization. I do not know if his dream will come true, but whenever I meet him I feel inspired and rejuvenated. His vision and jest for life is transformative. I salute his indomitable spirit.

28

An Inspirational Teacher

In my fairly long life spanning over seven decades, I have come in contact with many people of diverse character, temperament and background. Only some make a lasting impression on the mind and influence thinking and outlook while others flit through like passing shadows. Ramesh Babu was such an outstanding and memorable character, with whom I had the rare good fortune to come in close touch and whose memory I shall treasure forever.

After obtaining Post Graduate degree in History from the Calcutta University, I joined the West Bengal Education Service and was posted as a lecturer in History in Chunder Nagar, Government College. Chunder Nagar is a sub-division in Hooghly district in West Bengal and had been under French rule for a long time. The college I joined was known as the Duplex College named after the charismatic French ruler and general Duplex. The college building overlooking the river Ganges, unlike most other colleges of West Bengal, was spacious and well kept with huge columns and a beautiful patio. Strolling by the size of the river Ganges in the late afternoons was a grand and elevating experience soothing the soul and vitalizing the body. Rays of the setting sun falling on the flowing water used to create a magical atmosphere. Returning to the din and bustle of Calcutta at the end of the day was not a joyous experience.

Dr. Ramesh Mitra called by everyone as Ramesh Babu was the Head of the Department of History of the college. He was a renowned scholar and historian and commanded respect from all and one. He was a bachelor and a personification of simple living and high thinking. He was also a wonderful raconteur and used to tell us with a dry sense of humour many hilarious anecdotes of French rulers of Chundar Nagar and many other public figures of the days of yore. He had a prodigious memory and could describe events of the past with vivid details. I also gathered from him interesting tales of triumphs and tragedies, virtues and warts of well-known personalities of Bengal of pre-partition days and humorous asides linked with them. I also gleamed from him many stories of accomplishments as well as foibles of well-known academics of that period. His command over both English and French was phenomenal. He had also delved deep into the writings of Tagore and could recite flawlessly and without omitting a word some of his famous poems. He invariably spoke with great clarity and cogency. His erudition did not dazzle but exuded a soft and warm glow.

The students loved and respected him and he, in turn, showered on them his unbounded affection. While teaching in the college, I sat for the All India Services Examination and was selected for the Indian Police Service. I was somewhat disappointed as the police service had an unsavoury reputation and held few charms for me. My thinking was partly influenced by uncorroborated stories of police torture and brutality doing the rounds, particularly in the academic circles and the prevailing snootiness towards a service requiring more brawn than brain. I was indeed impaled on the horns of a dilemma and did not know whether to continue in education service or take up the challenge and opt for the rough and tumble of a police career. Many of my friends and relations compounded my misgivings by telling me that in police service, with my academic disposition, I shall be a square peg in a round hole and never be able to adjust myself to its requirements and end my career not in glory but ignominy.

However, there was one clear and reassuring voice. It was that of Ramesh Babu. His views reflected his clear and prescient mind. He told me that the police service would provide me, if I can cultivate a correct outlook, unique opportunities of helping and serving people, particularly the poor and disadvantaged at critical and crisis situations—an opportunity that very few other professions would provide. The power of the police are often being abused and misused, giving the profession a demoniac odour and imparting to police men the image of bogey men. The country needs young officers with character and compassion to make a clean break with the past. Helping and safeguarding the poor and disadvantaged people will give one a rare sense of satisfaction and fulfilment at the end of the day.

During my thirty five years of service in the police and few years in the National Human Rights Commission, I kept the counsel of the scholar-idealist in mind and felt influenced and inspired by what he had told me. To me, Ramesh Babu will always remain a moral beacon and a constant source of inspiration. I do not know how far I have succeeded in fitting this ideal with reality. I must have failed or faltered on many occasions. But these words always ring in my ears and have consciously or unconsciously influenced, in a large measure, my thinking and action in my career in law enforcement.

29

Expectations Unfulfilled

My first impression of Inspector S. Mohanty was not very flattering. He was Inspector in charge of Sadar Circle of Cuttack district, Odisha, when I was posted as an Assistant Superintendent of Police. Tall, bespectacled with a weather-beaten face and slow in movements, he was an antithesis of a go getting police officer. In the crime meetings, the Superintendent of Police used to tick him off for failing to exercise adequate control and supervision over the subordinate investigating officers. The then Superintendent of Police, Cuttack, B.K. Mohapatra, came from the army and was a tough disciplinarian. Junior officers were in mortal dread of him. But at the same time, they knew that when chips were down, the SP would stand by them and not let them down.

However, soon Mohanty's personality and style of work impressed me. He was never obsequious and had the unpolice like characteristic of not running down his colleagues and make snide remarks about the seniors. He invariably carried a typewriter with him (Computers being unknown and unheard of at that time) and would type out the inspection and supervision notes on the spot. He also urged me to follow this practice so that instruction after spot visits or supervision of important cases were promptly received by the subordinates. Dispatching notes after returning to headquarters often gets delayed because the senior officers become preoccupied with other chores and memory starts playing tricks. Mohanty, though not a graduate, had a good command over English. His notes were also concise and to the point.

I remember the occasion when I had gone for inspection of a police station, which fell within the Sadar Circle, Mohanty the Circle Inspector, was naturally present during my inspection. Inspection of a police station is an important item of work of a senior police officer. Elaborate instruction, in the Police Manual as well as multitude of police orders and circulars exist for the guidance of officers for inspection of police stations. Police stations constitute the microcosm of the police world in the district and an important interface between the police and the community. It is a crowning pity that many senior police officers now-a-days, do not inspect police stations, and even when they do make perfunctory visits, inspection notes written by subordinate officers are signed and issued by them. They thus stand diminished before the subordinates. This brazen dereliction of duty saps the professional and moral competence of the police leaders and highlights their failure to set the house in order. Many omissions and commissions by subordinate officers go undetected.

During inspection, I had reasons to appreciate as well as admonish the officer-in-charge of the police station. Some local gentry had also come to meet me, and they, as perhaps pre-arranged by the officers, were fulsome in their appreciation of the efficient working of the officers and men of the police station.

Before departure, I asked the officer-in-charge for the bill of the expenditure incurred in connection with mine and my stenographer's boarding and lodging. He was most unwilling to submit a bill and said that visit of a senior officer in the police station was an occasion for joy and satisfaction for the staff and I should not shame him by insisting on payment of a niggling sum. But I, fresh from training at the police academy and with the police conduct rules ringing my ears, was insistent. At this juncture, Inspector Mohanty intervened. He took me aside and said something which till now rings in my ears. He said that he was venturing to tell me something which he would not be able to do when I become a Superintendent of Police. In measured words he said that whatever amount I would pay would not equal, the actual expenditure the officer had incurred; ASP's inspection visit was an important occasion and many outsiders come to meet and pay respects to the visiting officer. Some additional expenditure was unavoidable and inescapable. Instead of fretting and fuming for payment of a small sum, I may kindly bear in mind what the subordinate officers expect from the IPS officers, who constitute the leadership of the police that they would act as true leaders. They themselves would not soil their hands by accepting bribes in cases investigated by the police. They must defend the subordinates against extraneous pressures when they were right and come down heavily on them like a ton of bricks if they were found corrupt and remiss. Very often, subordinate staff get dismayed and demoralized when the senior officers abdicate their responsibilities and bite the dust to curry favour with the political masters and betray the trust the subordinates repose in them. Those friendly but stinging words of Inspector Mohanty even now ring in my ears and give me a sense of acute disquiet. In the eyes of the subordinate officers, many of us are indeed lost leaders, failing to live up to standards expected of us. Police subordinates click their heels and salute us and speak deferentially with tongue-in-cheeks, but in heart of hearts they feel that we are pitch-forked in the position of leaders by joining the Indian Police Service, without developing requisite moral qualities; we fail to function as just and capable commanders, who can enthuse and inspire their men.

Today, there is politicization of the police down the line. Junior officers have taken cues from their seniors and developed close nexus with the politicians in power. In consequence, the Indian police has become the ruling party's police. For this sorry state of affairs, the major brunt of responsibility must be borne by us — the senior police officers.

30
Caste Barriers

It was a warm and sultry evening. I was about to leave for the club to see a movie when a phone call came from Cuttack. It was the voice of the Inspector-General of Police. He told me that a devastating tornado had hit some villages in the neighbouring district of Keonjhar, causing heavy destruction of human lives and property. He wanted me to immediately rush to Keonjhar, which was at a distance of nearly 150 miles from my Range Headquarters to mobilize the police personnel and organize relief and rescue operations for the tornado affected village.

Hurriedly packing a bag, I left for Keonjhar within an hour. The journey was nightmarish. The winding ghat roads of the Sub-Division were in a bad state of disrepair and because of the rains they were slushy and slippery. The beautiful dark and deep forests on either side of the road looked grim and menacing in the darkness of the night. The wind howled and roared. Incessant rains spattered on the windscreen of the car, reducing visibility almost to nil. By God's grace I reached Keonjhar at midnight safe and sound. I found that several officers of the district including the S.P. and the District Magistrate had already left for the tornado-hit villages. The officers present at district headquarters were unaware of the extent of the devastation and loss of human lives caused by this massive calamity. All kinds of exaggerated rumours were afloat.

Early next morning I reached the scene of devastation, which was at a distance of nearly 30 miles from the district headquarters. It was a traumatic experience. About eleven villages had been razed to the ground as if a giant bulldozer had rolled over them. Trees had been uprooted, electric poles twisted and broken, and houses, both mud and mortar built, had just disappeared. The havoc caused by the elemental fury of the nature was to be seen to be believed. Dead bodies of human beings and carcasses of the animals were lying scattered. The villagers were dumb-founded and almost stupefied by the suddenness and magnitude of the calamity. Their eyes were dry. They had no more tears to shed. All they could do was to look at us with vacant and listless eyes, not knowing what to do. Groups of relief workers were moving about, but they too were at a loss and did not know how to go about their job.

The first task of the police officers and men was to arrange for the cremation of the dead bodies lying near the ruins of the broken houses. The putrid smell of the dead bodies was filling the air and deepening the sense of death and gloom all around. I advised my officers to seek the help of the villagers for the disposal of the dead bodies. But I was amazed to find that even in this hour of grim tragedy, when the devastating fury of nature had levelled down all distinctions between the high and the low, the rich and the poor, there was a distinct reluctance on the part of many of the villagers to lift the dead bodies and place them on the funeral pyres arranged by us. Because of their reluctance, this work had to be done by the police officers.

When I asked some of the passive on-lookers the reasons for their inexplicable reluctance to step forward and help the cremation of the dead bodies of their compatriots, they replied that they belonged to the upper Mahanta caste and hence cannot, and would not, bury the dead bodies of persons, as they had found out that some of them belonged to lower sub-castes. To me this was a revelation. Even this massive natural calamity, which uprooted trees, demolished houses and reduced everything to the ground, could not break the villagers' age-old caste prejudices and inhibitions which had a vice-like grip on their minds.

Index

[illegible] unprecedentedly [illegible] violation of human rights by the [illegible] agencies, but the [illegible] conduct of the investigation [illegible] must be [illegible] and above board [illegible] the police has to be [illegible] transparent manner [illegible] police officers cannot be trampled on. As head of [illegible] wing, my [illegible] to lead by example [illegible] some successful investigation of custodial torture and redressal of grievances of the victims by our officers. He insisted on surprise visits to prisons and lockups to preclude the scope for cover ups and window dressing. When the International Committee of Red Cross (ICRC) wanted to visit prisons and detention centres of Jammu and Kashmir, the Union Home Ministry expressed reservations and feared that these visits might [illegible] intrusive and expose the country to international [illegible] and opprobrium. The NHRC, however, was [illegible] the government to permit these visits. Indeed, this [illegible] approach helped ICRC to visit prisons and detention centres in Jammu and Kashmir. This [illegible] the cause of [illegible] and silenced [illegible] and criticisms.

Justice Venkatachaliah robustly upheld the independence and integrity of the Commission. NHRC was repeatedly urging the government to accede to the UN Convention against Torture [illegible] 1987. The Ministry of Home Affairs informed the Commission that the question of India becoming a signatory to the Convention was discussed in Chief Ministers' conference in 199[illegible] [illegible] majority of the Chief Ministers were found not in favour of India's accession to the Convention. In a powerful [illegible] memorandum to the government, Venkatachaliah [illegible] acceding to the Convention "*would signify to the world [illegible] to conduct ourselves in a manner that we have decided ourselves to be [illegible]*